THE HUNTERS AND THE HUNTED

The Hunters and the Hunted

The Elimination of German Surface Warships Around the World 1914–15

BRYAN PERRETT

Pen & Sword
MARITIME

First published in Great Britain in 2012 by
Pen & Sword Maritime
An imprint of
Pen & Sword Books Ltd
47 Church Street
Barnsley
South Yorkshire
S70 2AS

ISBN 978 1 84884 638 8

A CIP catalogue record for this book is available from the British
Library.

Typeset in 11.5pt Bembo by Mac Style, Beverley, East Yorkshire
Printed and bound in the UK by the MPG Books Group Ltd.

Pen & Sword Books Ltd incorporates the imprints of Pen & Sword
Aviation, Pen & Sword Maritime, Pen & Sword Military, Wharncliffe
Local History, Pen & Sword Select, Pen & Sword Military Classics, Leo
Cooper, Remember When, Seaforth Publishing and Frontline
Publishing

For a complete list of Pen & Sword titles please contact
PEN & SWORD BOOKS LIMITED
47 Church Street, Barnsley, South Yorkshire, S70 2AS, England
E-mail: enquiries@pen-and-sword.co.uk
Website: www.pen-and-sword.co.uk

Contents

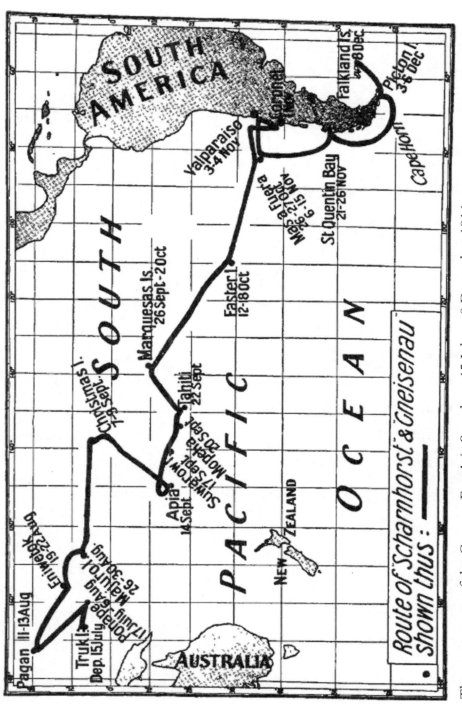

The movements of the German East Asia Squadron, 15 July to 8 December 1914.

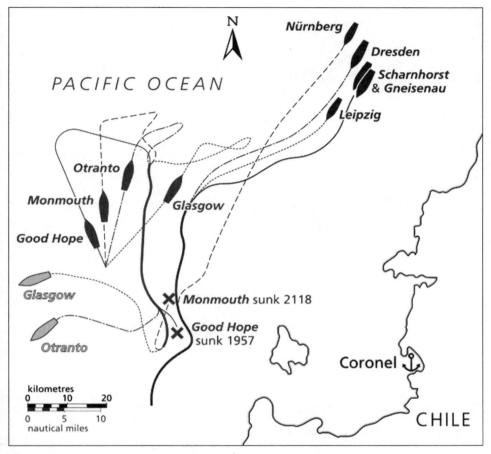

The Battle of Coronel, 1 November 1914.

The Battle of the Falkland Islands.

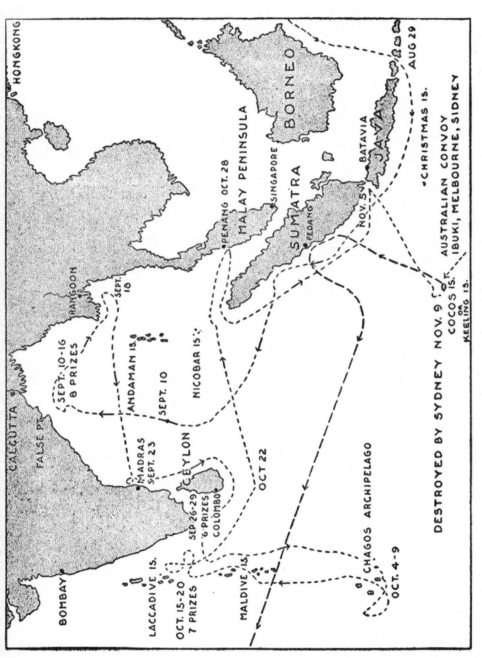

Escape route of *Emden*'s landing party from Cocos Island to the Red Sea — — — — — —
Cruise of the *Emden* — — — — — — — —

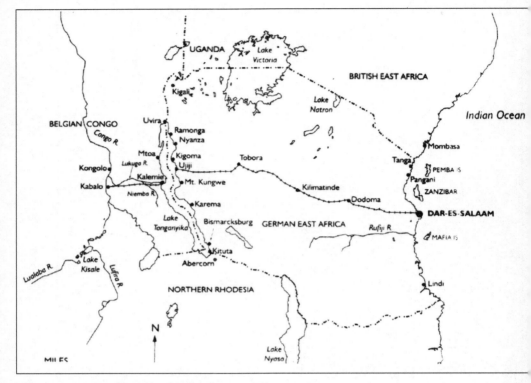

German East Africa and Lake Tanganyika.

Introduction

This is a story of ships and men, of battles fought a hundred years ago on the major oceans of the world, battles largely forgotten or unheard of that formed part of a war between empires vanished long since. When war between Great Britain and Imperial Germany began to seem inevitable the German Admiralty gave considerable thought as to how best British mercantile traffic could be damaged. The High Seas Fleet, built at enormous cost, was in any event designed purely for operations in the North Sea and the Baltic and quite unsuited to the *guerre de course*. The U-boat arm was in its infancy and the number of boats at its disposal was initially small. Again, its activities rarely extended beyond the North Sea, the English Channel, the Western Approaches to the United Kingdom and the Mediterranean Sea. On the other hand, Germany possessed colonies dotted around the world and these provided bases for surface warships. These consisted mainly of cruisers, but there were also a number of gunboats that would provide the armament for passenger liners that were earmarked for service with the Imperial Navy. The major problem involved was to keep regular and auxiliary warships supplied with coal. Colliers were chartered and supplies purchased close to where they would be needed. Inevitably, the German raiders would be operating in a climate of secrecy and an ingenious system was devised in which warships would replenish their fuel in coded grid-squares in remote ocean areas. In this way they were able to remain at sea for long periods, supplementing these supplies with more fuel and provisions taken from their victims.

Naturally, this course of action was predicted and allowed for by the British Admiralty in its dispositions. The Royal Navy of 1914 was the largest and most powerful in the world, yet its opponents enjoyed a number of advantages. Most of the Royal Navy, including its largest and most modern warships, was concentrated in the Grand Fleet at Scapa Flow in anticipation of a major clash in the North Sea with the German High Seas Fleet. That meant that despite its numerous bases in British colonies and dominions around the world the Royal Navy was required to police the world's oceans with comparatively few ships in relation to the vast areas involved. This not only required widespread dispersion, but also prolonged employment for its older ships, some of which were on the verge of retirement. It therefore did not follow that in any engagement between British and German cruisers the former would always enjoy numerical and qualitative advantages. It also meant that the Germans enjoyed the benefit of surprise and were able to strike at targets of their choice without warning. At the outbreak of war, for example, most people would have regarded the idea of a German cruiser bombarding Madras on the coast of India as being absurd. Thus, when it actually happened, the shock involved was the greater. Another factor which worked to Germany's advantage was that, with the exception of troop convoys, the Admiralty refused to introduce a system of escorted ocean convoys until May 1917. Until then, merchantmen made individual sailings, just as they had in peacetime, and were easy prey for the raiders. The provision of a single gun on the poop deck as defensive armament did little to deter the raiders with their multiple armament, although some British masters chose to make a fight of it, with inevitable results, although in one such engagement the raider was so battered that she came close to joining her victim on the bottom.

This, however, was a war in which those who hunted merchantmen were themselves being hunted by Allied warships. By the middle of 1915 all of Germany's pre-war cruisers that had been stationed abroad had been sunk or neutralised. They had, however, given a good account of themselves, sinking three British cruisers, one Russian cruiser and a French destroyer, as well as an impressive tonnage of merchant ships and their cargoes. Their loss was, of course, regretted in Germany, where it was decided that their work would be continued by commerce raiders. These were usually converted merchantmen armed with concealed guns and they possessed the ability to disguise their appearance with dummy funnels, upperworks, masts and foreign identities. Some produced good results but others achieved little. Again, they were too few in number and too widely scattered across huge expanses of ocean to have had a decisive influence.

It might be remembered that the introduction to one of the filmed versions of Anthony Hope's novel *The Prisoner of Zenda* informed audiences that the story was set in a time when 'politics had not outgrown the waltz and history still wore a rose'. Of course such an era never existed although the concept was pleasant enough. Nevertheless, unlike some aspects of the maritime war, this particular area of operations was conducted in a notably chivalrous spirit and in accordance with the life-saving traditions of the sea. Killing could not be avoided altogether, but it was never wanton. Unless sea conditions and the tactical situation prevented it, the crews and passengers of sunken ships were accommodated and received decent if confined treatment until their numbers grew to the extent that raider captains had to send them into a neutral port aboard one of his captures.

What makes the story so interesting is the manner in which the various characters involved reacted to the situations in which they found themselves, a point recognised immediately by writers of fiction such as C.S. Forester and Wilbur Smith. Careers were ruined because the German warships *Goeben* and *Breslau* were permitted to escape into Turkish waters. Vice Admiral von Spee believed that the business of the Imperial Navy was fighting battles and not making war on merchant ships. He got his wish, winning one engagement and losing another. Rear Admiral Sir Christopher Cradock was a prisoner of his Navy's tradition that a fight against odds should not be avoided and at Coronel he lost his life and two cruisers because of it. Vice Admiral Sir Doveton Sturdee had once refused to spy on a brother officer for Sir John Fisher and incurred the latter's lifelong spite because of it. Fisher even attempted to deny him any public credit, despite his having destroyed the enemy's East Asia Squadron at the Battle of the Falklands, to the extent of trying to prevent him attending an audience at which he was to receive the King's personal congratulations. Several of the German raider captains, notably von Müller of the *Emden,* Count Dohna-Schlodien of the *Mowe* and Felix von Luckner of the converted windjammer *Seeadler,* would have made very successful pirates in another era.

Bryan Perrett, April 2011

CHAPTER 1

Turkish Delight

For much of the nineteenth century the Turkish Empire was known as the Sick Man of Europe. During the early years of the twentieth century it had become increasingly apparent that the sickness had reached its terminal stage. The rule of Constantinople over large areas of North Africa had become purely nominal while elsewhere the stirring of nascent nationalism and conflicting racial and religious beliefs provided a background in which further fragmentation seemed inevitable. Even old friends such as Great Britain and France seemed to be turning against her when, together, they formed an Entente with Russia, Turkey's ancient and bitter enemy. In 1909 the autocratic Sultan Abdul the Damned was deposed in favour of his brother, who became Sultan Mohammed V. The new ruler was, in fact, little more than a figurehead, described as 'a spider blinking in unaccustomed sunlight' whenever he made one of his rare excursions beyond the palace walls. The real power lay with a group of progressive revolutionaries known as the Young Turks.

Other nations were quick to take advantage of Turkey's weakness. Her 1911-12 war with Italy resulted in her losing Libya, the Dodecanese Islands and Rhodes. In 1912-13 two wars against her Balkan neighbours reduced her once-considerable European holdings to a mere toehold. These defeats led the Young Turks to request German assistance in reorganising and training her army. In fact, German influence within the Turkish Empire had been growing steadily for a number of years and had, in many areas, replaced that of Great Britain.

This was a policy of which the German Emperor, Wilhelm II, thoroughly approved. It provided a potential ally in the event of war with Russia, which would be denied access to the Mediterranean via the Bosporus and Dardanelles, and concentrate British thoughts on the security of their own Imperial lifeline, the Suez Canal. He had made state visits to Abdul the Damned in 1889 and 1898 during which he insisted upon being addressed as Haji Mohammed Guillermo. This may have impressed the credulous but the more intelligent of his hosts would simply have acknowledged such an absurdity with oriental courtesy. Indeed, to have earned the title Haji he would have had to have made the pilgrimage to Mecca, which, as a Christian, was forbidden to him. Likewise, the name Mohammed had no place in his usual string of titles and the use of the Mediterranean version of Wilhelm was condescending, to say the least. Even stranger was a claim that somewhere in his family tree was the Prophet's daughter Fatima. However, those of his entourage who were familiar with the Kaiser's odd ways were prepared to tolerate them for the sake of the international prestige of the Imperial power that Germany had become.

Turkey had already benefited from the German connection. With mainly German money and engineering expertise, a railway was projected from Scutari on the shore of the Bosporus to Baghdad in Mesopotamia, with a further extension to Basra under consideration. By 1914 good progress had been made but some 300 miles of the central section still had to be constructed. Initially the British government had no objection to the project, but when the line came to be called the Berlin–Baghdad Railway it was clear that German strategic ambitions extended to the oilfields of the Persian Gulf, and this at a time when the Royal Navy was about to switch from coal to oil firing. In addition, a German presence in Basra, uncomfortably close to the shipping routes to Great Britain's Far Eastern colonies, would have been far from welcome. A second strategic rail route, the Hejaz Railway, ran from Damascus through Syria and down through Arabia to Medina. This was uncomfortably close to another British imperial artery, the Red Sea, and could be used to support military and naval forces capable of preying on this. Completed in the years prior to the outbreak of the Great War, the line ran at a profit made from pilgrims to Mecca, but subsequently provided a fine target for Colonel T.E. Lawrence and his Arab irregulars.

In 1914 naval contacts still existed between Great Britain and the Turkish Empire. The British naval mission in Constantinople still advised the ramshackle Turkish Navy, much of which dated from the previous century, and two of the most modern dreadnought battleships in the world were being built in British yards for Turkey. One, *Sultan Osman I*, had originally been ordered by Brazil and then transferred to Turkey. The second, *Rashadieh*, had been ordered by Turkey from the outset. These ships would mark the beginning of the Turkish Navy's modernisation programme and become the pride of fleet when they were delivered. The general public in particular took great pride in their purchase and was keenly awaiting their arrival.

On 2 August 1914 Germany signed an alliance with Turkey, which at this stage did not commit the latter to immediate military action. By now it was apparent that Great Britain would be at war with Germany in a matter of days at most, and the following day both dreadnoughts were requisitioned by the Royal Navy under the respective names of *Agincourt* and *Erin*. In Turkish eyes, her former ally and friend had betrayed her. Baron von Wangenheim, the German ambassador to the Turkish Empire, took full advantage of the anti-British feeling that was spreading throughout the country, offering to transfer the two warships of Germany's Mediterranean Squadron, the *Goeben* and the *Breslau*, to the Turkish Navy.

Goeben was a battle cruiser; a new class of warship that combined the hitting power of a battleship with the speed of a cruiser but possessed only limited protection. Her main armament consisted of ten 11-inch guns and her maximum speed was 28.4 knots. Like all German battle cruisers she was named after a successful military commander, in this case General August Karl von Goeben, who had distinguished himself in the Franco-Prussian War. *Breslau*, armed with twelve 4.1-inch guns and capable of 30 knots, was, like the majority of German cruisers, named after a town. The two ships had been showing the flag for Imperial Germany since 1912 and since then had visited eighty ports around the Mediterranean. Since 23 October 1913 the squadron had been commanded by Rear Admiral Wilhelm Souchon.

Following the assassination of Archduke Franz Ferdinand of Austria on 28 June 1914, Souchon sensed that diplomatic damage control measures would fail and that a full-scale European war had become inevitable. He took *Goeben* into the Austrian naval base of Pola in the Adriatic for urgent repairs to her boilers, which required no less than 4,460 of their tubes replacing, then sailed for Taranto, where he was joined by *Breslau*, which had been operating in the eastern Mediterranean. The two coaled at Messina, then sailed westward with the intention of intercepting French troop convoys leaving North Africa for France.

The protection of troop convoys leaving France's North African colonies was also to the fore in British minds. Winston Churchill, then First Lord of the Admiralty, despatched the following signal to the commander of the Royal Navy's Mediterranean Fleet, Admiral Sir Berkeley Milne:

> You are to aid the French in the transportation of their African Army by covering, and if possible, bringing to action individual fast German ships, particularly *Goeben,* who may interfere with that action. *Do not at this stage be brought to action against superior forces, except in combination with the French, as part of a general battle.* [author's italics]

The Mediterranean Fleet, based at Malta, consisted of three battle cruisers (*Inflexible, Indefatigable* and *Indomitable*), four armoured cruisers, four light cruisers and fourteen destroyers. Its principle defect lay in its commander, a former Groom-in-Waiting to the late King Edward VII. He had spent a great deal of his time aboard the Royal Yacht and was generally believed to have received his present appointment because of his qualities as a courtier. A good man to have at a party, one of his more memorable asides was that he had never disobeyed an order and never used his discretion. As the reverse constituted part of the Nelson Touch, its absence was to prove disastrous in the present circumstances.

By 3 August *Goeben* and *Breslau* were off the coast of French North Africa. Shortly after dawn next day *Goeben* carried out a brief bombardment of Philipville (now Skikda) while *Breslau* shelled Bone (now Annaba). The orders that Souchon had received direct from the Kaiser now permitted him to break out into the Atlantic and return home, at his discretion. Such a course of action would almost certainly have resulted in the loss of both ships, but unknown to the Kaiser fresh secret orders were received from Grand Admiral Alfred von Tirpitz and the German Admiralty to the effect that he should head eastwards immediately and make for Constantinople.

Having learned that the German ships had headed west after leaving Messina, Milne despatched *Indomitable*, *Indefatigable* and the light cruiser *Dublin* after them. At 09.30 on 4 August they encountered them, approaching on an opposite course. The usual compliments were not exchanged and the British ships swung round behind their quarry, with *Indomitable* and *Indefatigable* sailing parallel to each other so that *Goeben's* fire would be split if the chase developed into a fight. That began to seem less and less likely when the Cabinet refused permission until the British ultimatum to Germany expired at midnight. Meanwhile, *Goeben* and *Breslau* began to pull further and further ahead until they vanished below the horizon. Because of her boiler problems *Goeben* had only been able to work up to 24 knots and to achieve this Souchon extended the usual two-hour shifts in the stokeholds to four hours. The stokers' frenzied labour at the roaring furnaces, rendered twice as hard by the tropical Mediterranean summer, killed four of them with heatstroke or scalding.

While the British battle cruisers had been unable to keep up, the cruiser *Dublin* managed to maintain contact until the evening when, in mist and fading light, she lost sight of the Germans off Cape San Vito on the north coast of Sicily. With the threat removed, Souchon sailed into Messina once more and began coaling from the German merchant ships in the harbour. Now that a war situation existed, the Italians, being neutral, insisted that he left with twenty-four hours of his arrival, but even with the assistance of 400 volunteers from the merchantmen, the decks of which had to be ripped open for the sake of speed, only 1,500 tons of coal could be transferred by the evening of 6 August. Even that addition was insufficient to take *Goeben* and *Breslau* as far as Constantinople, forcing Souchon to make arrangements for a rendezvous with a collier among the Aegean islands.

At this point the German admiral received two depressing messages from Tirpitz. The first was that as a state of war did not exist between Great Britain and the Austro-Hungarian Empire at that time and in the circumstances the Austrian Navy could not provide assistance for German operations in the Mediterranean. That meant that Souchon could not rely on seeking refuge in the Austrian naval base at Pola in the Adriatic without exposing his ships to the risk of temporary internment being trapped in this backwater for the duration of the war when Austria did declare war, as was fully expected. A second signal informed him that as Turkey was also still neutral, Constantinople was denied to him for identical reasons. However, Souchon had no intention of becoming some sort of *Flying Dutchman* and decided to head for Constantinople anyway, thereby forcing the Turks, whether they liked it or not, to extend the naval war into the Black Sea, where they could attack the Russians. This was not altogether wishful thinking, but some diplomatic jiggery-pokery would be needed to place his ships beyond the reach of the Royal Navy.

Meanwhile, Milne deployed *Inflexible* and *Indefatigable* to close the northern exit from the Straits of Messina, while *Indomitable* was despatched to coal at Bizerta, on the north-east coast of Tunisia. He was absolutely convinced that Souchon's plans still centred on attacking the French transports or breaking out into the Atlantic, the result being that his three battle cruisers were so far from the scene of future events that they unable to play any significant role. Elsewhere, the light cruiser *Gloucester* under Captain Howard Kelly covered the southern exist from the Straits of Messina. The entrance to the Adriatic was patrolled by Rear Admiral Emest Troubridge's 1st Cruiser Squadron consisting of the armoured cruisers *Defence*, *Black Prince* and *Duke of Edinburgh*, reinforced with the light cruiser *Dublin*.

In the event, the Italians were kinder to Souchon than they should have been, permitting him to remain in Messina for a total of thirty-six hours. When he left on 6 August he made for the southern exit from the Straits into the Eastern Mediterranean, where he was immediately detected by *Gloucester*. He then turned north as though he was heading into the Adriatic with Pola as his destination. *Gloucester* shadowed him and Howard Kelly transmitted a warning to Troubridge that the enemy was heading his way.

Troubridge was firmly convinced that the Germans *were* heading for Pola. He took his four cruisers north from his current position, off Corfu, in what he believed was an interception course. Howard Kelly suddenly reported that shortly after dark *Goeben* and *Breslau* had changed course and were now heading south-east to round Cape Matapan on the south coast of Greece. Troubridge considered this to be a feint and maintained his northerly course until 01.00, when *Gloucester* reported that the enemy were still on their south-easterly course and that she had exchanged shots with *Breslau*. Only then did Troubridge, unable to send his destroyers in pursuit because they were low on fuel, reverse his own course in a vain attempt to catch up.

Aboard *Defence* with Troubridge was his Flag Captain, Fawcett Wray, who had a reputation as being a gunnery expert but whose character somewhat resembled that of Iago in Shakespeare's *Othello*. At 02.45 Wray asked Troubridge whether it was his intention to engage *Goeben* and *Breslau*. The Admiral replied that it was, then referred to the Admiralty's instruction not to engage a superior force, commenting that he knew he would be doing wrong, but he was not prepared to destroy to good name of the Mediterranean Fleet by not doing so. This was not the answer Wray wanted to hear. Three-quarters of an hour later he raised the subject again, remarking that he was not looking forward to the prospect of fighting as powerful a ship as the *Goeben*. Troubridge expressed his agreement, at which Wray pressed his argument: 'I don't see what you can do, sir. The *Goeben* can circle round us within range of her guns but outside ours. It seems likely to be the suicide of your squadron.'

This, of course, was nonsense and was proved to be so in December 1939 when Commodore Henry Harwood, with the cruisers *Ajax*, *Achilles* and *Exeter*, took on and defeated the much stronger German pocket battleship *Admiral Graf Spee* simply by attacking from different directions and dividing the enemy's fire.

Troubridge, however, seems to have been convinced and replied: 'I cannot turn away now; think of my pride.' Wray knew that he had won his point and his riposte bordered on the insolent: 'Has your pride anything to do with it, sir? Surely it is your country's welfare that is at stake.' In reality, the chances of an engagement were non-existent as the 1st Cruiser Squadron was now some 70 miles behind the faster *Goeben* and stood no chance at all of catching her. Troubridge may have sensed this and known that his initial turn to the north had created a situation for which he would be held responsible; he would also have to justify his apparent willingness to shirk an engagement with the enemy. His otherwise blameless career, he knew, was in ruins. At 03.55, with tears running down his cheeks, he gave the order for the chase to be abandoned, then informed Milne of his decision. 'This is the bravest thing you have ever done,' was Wray's inscrutable comment.

In the meantime, others had come close to catching the Germans. At 14.00 the previous afternoon the *Dublin* and two destroyers had left Malta with the intention of joining Troubridge. At 20.30 Captain John Kelly, Howard Kelly's brother and commander of the *Dublin*, received orders direct from Milne to launch a torpedo attack on the enemy, using *Gloucester's* shadowing reports as guidance. Howard Kelly expected to sight *Goeben* at about 03.30, but by the worst possible luck was himself spotted by *Breslau's* lookouts. Souchon therefore turned away and slid past the British ships to starboard without being seen.

Howard Kelly in *Gloucester* continued to shadow the Germans on the morning of 8 August. He received a signal from Milne telling him to 'drop astern and avoid capture', which he chose to ignore. Instead, his idea was to give *Breslau* a mauling so that *Goeben* would come to her assistance and then be engaged by other British ships taking part in the pursuit. At 13.35 *Gloucester* opened fire on *Breslau* at 11,500 yards and the latter replied. Souchon reported that *Breslau* sustained a hit, which seems to have caused very little damage, and, as Kelly had hoped, went to her assistance until *Gloucester* retreated out of range. Kelly was quite happy to continue with this game, disregarding his Commander-in-Chief's instructions not to proceed east of Cape Matapan, but at 16.40 a fuel shortage compelled him to turn away.

Once again, luck came to Souchon's assistance. Back in London, a clerk at the Admiralty returned from lunch to find a swatch of telegrams awaiting despatch on a colleague's desk. Helpfully, he decided to despatch them himself. Unfortunately, that addressed to Milne was worded 'Commence hostilities against Austria' and should not have been sent until 12 August, the date upon which the British ultimatum to the Austro-Hungarian Empire expired. Upon receipt of the signal Milne, now heading eastwards with his three battle cruisers and an additional light cruiser, decided to ignore developments in the Eastern Mediterranean and turned north into the Adriatic to support Troubridge. Back at the Admiralty scenes of near hysteria followed the discovery of the mistake. Four hours after receipt of the first signal Milne received its successor, cancelling it. The Admiralty, however, left him with the impression that the situation could alter at very short notice and he continued to press on into the Adriatic. It was not until 12.30 on 9 August that the position was clarified with a third signal: 'Not at war with Austria. Continue chase of *Goeben*.'

As a full day had been wasted it was now far too late to do anything about the *Goeben* and *Breslau*. Their voyage up the Aegean took on the aspect of a pleasure cruise, punctuated by the need to coal off the island of Denusa. Souchon's only anxiety was whether the Turks would permit him to enter the Dardanelles. He need not have worried, for Enver Pasha, the Turkish Minister of War, had cleared the way for him. Even as the funnel smoke from Milne's resumed pursuit appeared above the southern horizon, at 17.00 on 10 August the Germans were met by a Turkish pilot boat at the entrance to the straits, through which they were guided to the Sea of Marmara. From there it was plain sailing to receive the warmest of welcomes at Constantinople.

Milne, furious, sent the light cruiser *Weymouth* to the mouth of the Dardanelles to remind the Turks that the German warships should be sent out within twenty-four hours of their arrival. The bland response was that there were no German warships in Turkish waters. Fierce arguments to the contrary were met with the smiling response that two German warships had reached Constantinople, but had since been purchased by the Turkish government. They were now part of the Sultan's navy and had been given new names: *Goeben* had become the *Yavuz Sultan Selim* and *Breslau* had been renamed *Medili*. Members of the British naval mission and Constantinople Embassy staff verified that on visiting the city's famous harbour, the Golden Horn, crowds of delighted Turks were assembling daily to admire their navy's latest acquisition, from the sterns of which hung the red Turkish ensign with its distinctive white sickle moon and star. On their decks German officers could be identified, despite have replaced their peaked caps with the fez. The press was full of praise for Souchon's achievement, announcing that he was now Commander-in-Chief of the Turkish Navy.

It quickly became apparent that Turkey was responding favourably to German overtures for an alliance. On 15 August the Royal Navy's mission was informed that its services were no longer required and it left Constantinople a month later. On 27 September Weber Pasha, the German officer responsible for the security of the Dardanelles, declared that the straits were closed to all shipping. This blocked Russia's exit from the Black Sea, used for 90 per cent of import and export business. On 29 October Souchon led a squadron, including the former *Goeben* and *Breslau*, into the Black Sea and bombarded three major Russian ports. On 2 November Russia declared war on Turkey, followed by Great Britain and France four days later. The Sultan's announcement that this was a holy war met with little enthusiasm in some parts of his empire; the Sherif of Mecca, a man of immense influence throughout the Muslim world, disagreed and started a rebellion in Arabia.

Meanwhile, what of those who had permitted the two German ships to escape to Turkey? Milne, Troubridge and Wray were summoned to England and required to explain their actions. Milne appeared to have escaped censure but was later informed that he would not be taking up the prestigious appointment of command at the Nore, which had been promised to him and was not employed at sea again. Troubridge was charged that 'he did forbear to chase His Imperial German Majesty's ship *Goeben*, being an enemy then flying,' but was exonerated although he was not employed at sea again. His final appointment was to command a number of naval guns landed to support the Serbian Army. He maintained that but for Wray's advice he would have fought the *Goeben*, but in the final analysis the decision not to fight devolved upon him alone. Wray claimed that he had been misunderstood and 'was astounded when Troubridge announced his intention of abandoning the chase.' Ostracised by his fellow naval officers, his career was finished. Only the two Kelly brothers, John and Howard, emerged with credit from the affair, the latter being awarded the Companionship of the Bath for his tenacious pursuit of the German ships. His name was also commemorated by the destroyer *Kelly*, commanded by Lord Louis Mountbatten in the Second World War.

As for the *Goeben* and *Breslau*, they took part in numerous operations against the Russian Black Sea Fleet, but will appear again in this story. Writing *of Goeben*, Winston Churchill commented that 'For the peoples of the Middle East [she] carried more slaughter, more misery and more ruin than has ever before been borne within the compass of a ship.' Because *of Goeben*, Turkey became Germany's ally in a world war. Yet Turkey had recently been defeated by her smaller Balkan neighbours and Italy, so how could she hope to stand against the might of the British Empire, even with German assistance. When the war ended, she had lost Arabia, Palestine, Syria and Mesopotamia and over 300,000 of her people were dead. In 1922 the Sultanate was abolished and the remnant of the ancient Ottoman Empire became a republic.

CHAPTER 2

Lost – Cause Unknown

Give or take the odd hurricane, the Caribbean and what had once been called the Spanish Main was a grand station for a warship to be based. Together with the South American coast, it produced a huge and varied trade with Europe that justified the presence of cruisers to safeguard the interests of their respective nationalities and show the flag. It was a place of spread deck awnings, white tropical uniforms, and a social life in which the most important of the local residents, their wives and daughters were entertained aboard and reciprocated with hospitality ashore. All in all, now that tropical diseases were being brought under control, it was a pleasant place to be with an enjoyable climate. There was always, however, a sinister aspect to life in many of the countries bordering the Caribbean in that violence was an endemic quality of their political lives. In some of the smaller states that no longer had connections with a European power, the United States acted as sort international policeman until order had been restored. Generally, the colonial powers provided stability within their own colonies and actually cooperated in looking after each other's interests.

There was one country that no one was capable of policing or providing any sort of stability, and that was Mexico. On 25 May 1911 President Diaz was overthrown, his place being taken by Francisco Madero. Not everyone liked Madero and a civil war broke out, ending when he was defeated and killed by Victoriano Huerta on 22 February 1913. Again, not many people liked Huerta, who instituted so harsh a rule that the United States government simply refused to recognise him. Internal opposition, led by Venustiano Carranza and others with similar ambitions, quickly resulted in armed revolution, while armed bandit gangs took on the guise of private armies and did exactly what they liked.

His Imperial Majesty's light cruiser *Dresden,* under the command of Captain Erich Kohler, arrived in the West Indies during the summer of 1913. Mexico's troubles reached epic proportions in April 1914 when several unarmed American sailors were arrested in Tampico. Following this the port of Vera Cruz was shelled by a United States naval task force which also landed sufficient troops to cover the evacuation of American civilians from the city. During this episode *Dresden* provided not only assistance but also transport for the recently deposed President Huerta, his family and closest supporters, who left Vera Cruz just as Carranza's men entered the city. They were not particularly welcome passengers and Kohler was pleased to set them ashore in Kingston, Jamaica, where the British authorities had granted them asylum.

Kohler was well known and liked throughout the Caribbean, notably among the international shipping community, but he also took in great interest in the Royal Navy and its methods of doing things. He would have met the commander of the North America and West Indies station, Rear Admiral Sir Christopher Cradock, and known most of his captains socially. Initially, Cradock's command consisted of the cruiser *Bristol,* joined by Fourth Cruiser Squadron containing the *Suffolk* (flag), *Berwick, Essex* and *Lancaster* because of the deteriorating situation in Mexico. Later, following the outbreak of war in Europe, they would be reinforced by Rear Admiral A.P. Stoddart's Fifth Cruiser Squadron: *Carnarvon* (flag), *Cornwall, Cumberland* and *Monmouth.* It might seem, therefore, that Cradock had a considerable force at his disposal with which to hunt a possible quarry, but it must be remembered that not only was it required to cover a vast area stretching from Halifax in Nova Scotia, Canada, to Pernambuco in Brazil, and that the numerous islands of the Caribbean had provided hiding places since the days of the buccaneers.

While the storm clouds of war gathered and grew ever darker, those aboard *Dresden* were looking forward to being relieved by Captain

Emil Luddecker's *Karlsruhe* and then returning home for a refit at Kiel and some leave. In fact, the relief took place at Port au Prince, Haiti, on 26 July and just days later, on the outbreak of war, their orders were changed. The two captains would exchange ships. *Dresden* would head south, round Cape Horn and rendezvous in the South Pacific with the light cruiser *Leipzig,* which had been safeguarding German interests off the west coast of Mexico, as well as Vice Admiral Count Maximilian von Spee's East Asiatic Squadron, which was setting out on its long voyage from Tsingtao, Germany's base in northern China. The arrangement would also enable Kohler to employ his extensive knowledge of Caribbean mercantile traffic to conduct a damaging cruiser war against Allied shipping, a context in which the necessary arrangements for supply ships and colliers had already been made.

There was no doubt that Kohler was pleased with his new command. Her two steam turbine engines were capable of producing a maximum speed of 27 knots that would enable her to outrun the older, larger and better armed cruisers that Cradock possessed, while her twelve 4.1-inch guns would enable her to hold her own against opponents of comparable size. Germany, like Great Britain, was requisitioning passenger liners for service as armed merchant cruisers and on 6 August *Karlsruhe* met the Norddeutscher Lloyd luxury liner *Kronprinz Wilhelm* at sea to assist in converting her to this role. Launched in 1901, in September the following year the *Kronprinz Wilhelm* had won the Blue Riband, crossing from Cherbourg to New York in five days, eleven hours and fifty-seven minutes with an average speed of 23.09 knots. In the same year she had carried the Kaiser's brother, Crown Prince Albert Wilhelm Heinrich von Preussen, together with a large press corps, on a state visit to New York, where he was received by President Theodore Roosevelt. Since then, her passenger list had included many famous names from the world of the stage and music, among them Oscar Hammerstein, and members of European and American society. The armament she now received from *Karlsruhe* included two 3.4-inch guns and 290 rounds of ammunition, a machine gun and thirty-six rifles. *Karlsruhe's* navigating officer, Lieutenant Commander Paul Thierfelder, became the liner's new captain while her merchant skipper, the former Captain Grahn, received a naval commission as his second-in-command. Two petty officers and thirteen ratings were also transferred to from the cruiser.

In return, *Kronprinz Wilhelm* transferred some of her coal to *Karlsruhe.* This operation had to be hastily abandoned when *Suffolk,* Cradock's flagship, appeared over the horizon. *Karlsruhe* headed north at speed while *Kronprinz Wilhelm* veered away to the north-north-east on the first leg of a varied course that would take her to the Azores. Cradock quickly reached the conclusion that he was unable to catch the faster German cruiser and made radio contact with two of his own ships, *Bristol* and *Berwick*, which were located along the course line that Kohler had set. *Bristol,* commanded by Captain B.H. Fanshawe, was on a reciprocal course to *Karlsruhe* and at 20.15 spotted her 6 miles distant, illuminated by a full moon. He swung *Bristol* on to a parallel course and opened fire at 7,000 yards. *Karlsruhe* replied but neither ship scored a hit in the gathering gloom. Kohler turned away eastwards and soon outpaced her opponent. By 22.30 *Bristol's* speed had dropped to 18 knots and she no longer had *Karlsruhe* in sight. There was a chance that *Berwick* might have intercepted the German cruiser at about 08.00 next morning, but at the critical moment she made an alteration of course which took her away from her quarry. However, when *Karlsruhe* entered San Juan harbour on the American island of Puerto Rico, the pursuit had cost her all but 12 tons of her precious coal.

The American authorities enforced the strict requirements of neutrality, informing Kohler that his ship must leave San Juan within twenty-four hours of her arrival. During this period he loaded sufficient coal to take him to Willemstad on the Dutch island of Curacao where he obtained a further supply which enabled him to make a rendezvous with one of his supply ships, the *Patagonia,* on 17 August. The following day *Karlsruhe* began a raiding career that rivalled that of *Emden,* her more famous cousin, by sinking the freighter *Bowes Castle*, the crew of which he transferred to the *Stadt Schleswig*, another of Kohler's supply ships, shortly after. On 28 August he was able to make good all his shortages off Fernando de Noronha where he met another three German supply ships.

For the next two months *Karlsruhe* ran riot around the West Indies, capturing and sinking no less than fifteen more ships, bringing her total of British shipping destroyed to 72,216 tons. During this period three factors were constantly to the forefront of Kohler's mind. These were the ever present need to acquire fuel, the constant danger posed by patrolling British warships and, of course, his primary mission of inflicting as much damaged as possible on the enemy's commerce. Regarding the last, from 20 September onwards he began operating with a supply ship positioned 20 miles distant on either beam to increase the radius of his search, the only German raider captain to employ this method of detecting possible kills.

On 14 September he was in the process of sinking the steamer *Highland Hope* when a Spanish merchantman came into view. Naturally, the Spaniard was curious and asked by radio what was happening. Kohler got his wireless operator to reply that he was part of a British convoy. This signal was intercepted by the British pre-dreadnought battleship *Canopus,* which had recently arrived on station. Those aboard *Canopus* would have known that the Admiralty was not in favour of convoys and their suspicions would have been aroused at once. She immediately asked the Spaniard for her position. The transmission alerted *Karlsruhe* to the fact that she might well be in some danger and Kohler gave the order for her to leave the area at maximum speed. Although he was unaware of the fact, *Canopus* was nearing the end of her useful life, and although her specification claimed that she was capable of up to 19 knots, long service had reduced that by a third and there was not the slightest chance of her being able to overhaul *Karlsruhe.* Against this, *Canopus* was invisible to *Karlsruhe* and Kohler was unaware of her precise range and position. On the other hand, if her call sign had been identified, Kohler's recognition manual would have told him that her main armament consisted of four 12-inch guns, and to a light cruiser that was very serious opposition indeed.

Kohler treated his captive crews according to international maritime law and sent them ashore on at least two occasions, the last being the despatch of *Crefeld,* one of his supply ships, to the Canary

Islands on 13 October. The raider's last capture was that of the 10,000-ton liner *Van Dyke,* on 28 October.

Next, Kohler decided to destroy the British radio station on Barbados. During the early evening of 4 November *Karlsruhe* was gliding smoothly across a flat sea when the entire forepart of the ship, including the bridge and the first funnel, were ripped apart by a huge explosion and sank immediately. That portion from the second funnel aft remained afloat but was sinking and did so within thirty minutes. The supply ships *Idrani-Hoffnung* and *Rio Negro* headed for the scene at speed and picked up *Karlsruhe's* survivors, of whom there were only 129. Kohler and over 250 of his men had been lost in the explosion and its immediate consequence. The cause of the disaster has never been fully explained. One cause commonly put forward is sweating cordite in the forward magazines. Another possibility is an explosion of coal dust, which was at its most dangerous in a hot, humid climate. In 1898 the American battleship *Maine* was lost to this cause in Havana harbour, and a secondary explosion in a coal bunker following a torpedo strike is widely regarded as contributing to the loss of the *Lusitania* in 1915.

The *Idrani-Hoffnung* was scuttled shortly after, while the *Rio Negro* set out on the voyage to Germany. Incredibly she worked he way through the British blockade and reached Norway. As she had clearly been engaged in hostilities, both the ship and the *Karlsruhe's* survivors were interned by the Norwegian authorities. They were, however, permitted to inform the German Admiralty of the details relating to the cruiser's loss. The Allies, while aware that *Karlsruhe* was no longer active in the Caribbean, remained in ignorance of her fate until March 1915 when wreckage attributable to her was discovered.

Merchant Vessels Sunk by the *Konigsberg* in 1914

Bowes Castle, 18 August
Strathroy, 31 August
Maple Branch, 3 September
Highland Hope, 14 September
Indrani, 17 September
Maria, 21 September
Cornish City, 21 September
Rio Iguazu, 22 September
Niceto de Larrinaga, 6 October
Lynrowan, 7 October
Cervantes, 8 October
Pruth, 9 October
Condor, 11 October
Glanton, 18 October
Hurstdale, 23 October
Van Dyke, 28 October

CHAPTER 3

Atlantic Rendezvous

The South American coast is 3,000 miles long and punctuated at frequent intervals by bays, inlets and river estuaries, all of which offer suitable hiding places for anyone wishing to conceal a vessel of even moderate size. In addition, there are two locations off the Brazilian coast that offer far less obvious hiding places, both being formed by the peaks of submarine mountain ranges. The first, lying 220 miles from the mainland, is Fernando Noranha and consists of a tiny archipelago the principal island of which, 7 miles long and 5 miles across, supports some 300 inhabitants. The second, approximately 400 miles further out into the Atlantic, is known as the Islhas de los Trinidade, and amounts to little more than a collection of huge jagged rocks. These are uninhabited and offer little more than an anchorage, a beach or two, some stunted vegetation and a freshwater spring. The problem was that these hiding places were so remote that this fact alone attracted them to a potential searcher and because of this the Islhas de los Trinidade were to become the scene of one of the most remarkable encounters in maritime history.

After exchanging captains with the *Karlsruhe*, the *Dresden* had headed south on the first leg of her journey to the Pacific. On 4 August she met the steamer *Baden*, which was carrying 6,000 tons of coal and became her personal collier. Two days later she stopped three British merchant ships, the *Drumcliffe*, *Lynton Grange* and *Hostilius*. Captain Ludecke has been accused of being insufficiently ruthless for total war, but it would be fairer to say that he was quite prepared to do his duty while retaining the values of a gentler age. In this case he released all three of his prizes; *Drumcliffe* because her passengers included women and children, and the other two because their cargos were of no use to the belligerent powers. No doubt his officers expressed concern that the recent captives would report the *Dresden's* presence at the first opportunity, but this did not alter his way of thinking. On 8 August he captured and sank the freighter *Hyades*, fully laden with a cargo of grain, but released the *Siamese Prince* on 16 August because her holds were empty. In the latter case Ludecke's boarding officer made his own feelings clear by inscribing the ship's log to the effect that he hoped that next time they met her holds would be full. Following this, Ludecke took *Dresden* to Fernando Noronha, where he anchored off the principal island to coal from the *Baden*.

This task completed he headed for Trinidade, where he found several colliers and the gunboat *Eber* (Boar) in the principal bay. *Eber*, under Commander Julius Wirth, was a small river gunboat armed with two 4.1-inch guns and six 37mm heavy machine guns. Her usual station was on the coast of German West Africa where there was little for her to do except curtail the activities of diamond smugglers as far as possible. Launched in 1903, she was sorely in need of a refit and was a frequent visitor to Cape Town where she was able to replace worn engineering parts. On the outbreak of war, Wirth was ordered to take her, accompanied by a supply ship, across the Atlantic to Trinidade and await further orders. The ocean voyage had not improved the condition of the tiny gunboat, the constant pitching and rolling starting several plates in her hull so that her bilge pumps were in continuous use. Thus, when Ludecke brought the immaculate *Dresden* into the bay he was confronted by the least reputable looking ship in the entire Imperial Navy, her hull streaked with rust, her decks still grubby from the additional coal she had been forced to carry during her long voyage, and a constant stream of dirty water spewing out of her bilges. Ludecke had no intention of remaining at Trinidade and left as soon as he had replenished his supplies, telling Wirth that for the moment his task was simply to guard the precious colliers assembled in the bay and await further orders. In the meantime, he pointedly sent several tins of paint across to the smaller vessel. A few days later *Eber* received fresh orders by radio message from *Dresden,* now many miles to the south. An armed merchant cruiser would be arriving at Trinidade shortly. Wirth was to transfer *Eber's* armament to her, take command, and prey on Allied shipping along the local trade routes. *Eber* was to be decommissioned as a unit of the Imperial Navy, make for Bahia Blanca in Brazil, and allow herself to be detained.

The armed merchant cruiser was the recently completed luxury liner *Cap Trafalgar,* flagship of the Hamburg South America Line, commanded by Captain Fritz Langerhannz, the company's senior captain. Her name might be considered to be unusual for a German liner, but had been conferred in the hope that she would attract British passengers. To this end her public rooms were decorated with portraits of Admiral Nelson, his mistress, his captains and paintings representing his ships and their various victories. Among her more unusual features was a sort of greenhouse at the after end of her superstructure. This was described as the Winter Garden and displayed various raised beds containing tropical plants, augmented by marble columns. When the war began she had just completed her maiden voyage to Buenos Aires and her chances of returning to Germany were remote. The Argentine authorities were far from helpful, but Langerhannz received what amounted to orders from a Lieutenant Commander Muller, who had recently taken up the post of German Naval Attaché in Buenos Aires, having travelled south from New York aboard the collier *Berwind.* He informed Langerhannz that the *Cap Trafalgar* was to be requisitioned as an armed merchant cruiser. For the moment Langerhannz would sail the ship and one of his reserve officers named Feddersen, nominated as First Lieutenant, would be responsible for fighting her. Langerhanz pointed out that the ship was unarmed, at which Muller said he would discuss the situation with the Admiralty in Berlin. Having done this he returned with more definite instructions. *Cap Trafalgar* would continue taking on fuel discretely, despite the attitude of the authorities; any shortfall of coal could be made good with railway sleepers. She would then leave without drawing attention to herself and drop down the River Plate to Montevideo in Uruguay, where the authorities were more kindly disposed. There, she would complete coaling and make up her crew numbers, replacing those reservists who had left the ship at Buenos Aires. Having completed these tasks, Langerhannz was ordered to take his command to Islhas de los Trinidade, where she would be supplied with guns.

During this period much was done to disguise the ship. No German liner on the South American route had more than two funnels. Her rearmost funnel, a dummy housing equipment that was easily relocated, was therefore taken down. The glass of the Winter Garden was painted white, leaving circles of clear glass to simulate portholes in a solid structure. The boot-topping was painted red to resemble that of Cunarders, while the two remaining funnels were painted black-over-red, which were also the Cunard colours. In this way the *Cap Trafalgar* now bore a remarkable resemblance to the Cunard liner *Carmania*, which had also been requisitioned as an armed merchant cruiser. There were, however, some notable differences. Battleship grey paint now covered the latter's hull, superstructure and funnel, while her boot-topping had been over-painted in black.

In peacetime *Carmania* was commanded by Captain James Clayton Barr, one of Cunard's most senior captains who would become Commodore of the line. Now aged fifty-nine, Barr was of short stature but his eyes indicated a shrewd knowledge of the sea, ships and men gained during a lifetime afloat. He had first gone to sea in 1877, serving in sail and before the mast before gaining his officer's ticket. As a teenager he had rounded the Horn several time and been involved in three shipwrecks. Having graduated to steam he joined Cunard as a junior deck officer and his upward progress to master had been rapid. Prior to taking over *Carmania* in 1905 he had commanded several of Cunard's better known liners, including the *Mauretania*. Such was his skill at handling his 19,000-ton command that he was able to dispense with the use of tugs when berthing or leaving harbour, thereby saving his employers a considerable bill and earning himself a bonus.

He had first come to the public's attention in 1913 when, on 10 October, he had answered a call for assistance from the immigrant liner *Volturno*, on fire and battling a gale in the mid–Atlantic. When the fire began to gain ground, several lifeboats were launched with disastrous consequences. Some were swamped or capsized in the heavy seas, while others were smashed against the ship's hull as they were being lowered, pitching their occupants into the water below. Some 120 lives were lost in this way.

The *Carmania* was first to arrive, followed by nine more ships of various types. Barr took control, instructing the rescuers to circle the burning ship to avoid collisions while he illuminated the scene with his searchlights throughout the night. Some of the rescue ships launched their own lifeboats but very few of those aboard the *Volturno* were willing to jump into wild, bone-chilling waves below. Those aboard the stricken vessel were now confined to the after part of the ship. Shortly before dawn *Volturno* was shaken by a heavy internal explosion. It was now felt that it would not be long before she foundered but shortly after the oil tanker *Narrangansett* reached the scene and discharged part of her cargo on to the water, calming it sufficiently for the lifeboats to complete their tasks. Altogether, 520 passengers and crew were rescued. As the day wore on it became apparent that while *Volturno* had been reduced to a burned-out hulk, she refused to sink and therefore represented a serious hazard to navigation. A party was therefore sent aboard to open her sea cocks and she finally slid to the bottom. Several members of *Carmania's* crew, including Captain Barr, received awards for gallantry in respect of their actions during the rescue. *Carmania* had been Liverpool bound and on 27 October was mentioned in *The New York Times* on completion of her return trip: 'The Cunard liner *Carmania* arrived yesterday from Liverpool with forty-three survivors from the *Volturno*, including twenty-two women and children who had been rescued by the Leyland steamship *Devonian* and landed at Liverpool.'

The onset of war did not please Barr at all. He got on well with his German passengers and on his most recent trip to New York had particularly enjoyed the company of a Lieutenant Commander Muller. It would be too much to believe in this strange story of coincidences that this officer was not the same Lieutenant

Commander Muller who had given the *Cap Trafalgar* her orders in Buenos Aires, who is known to have recently arrived there from New York. Be that as it may, Barr had a far more personal reason for being averse to a major war, and that was the fact that he would lose command of his ship to a regular Royal Navy officer. Cunard had an agreement with the Admiralty that if the need arose she could be 'taken up from trade' as the saying goes, and to that end traverse rings had been built into her deck to house the eight 4.7-inch guns with which she was about to be armed as a merchant cruiser. There would, of course, be much else to do before the ship could set out on her new role, including the fitting of armour plate to vulnerable areas and the replacement of older or unsuitable crew members by Royal Navy and Royal Marine personnel and the stripping out of passenger cabins.

The ship was taken over by her new commander, Captain Noel Grant, on 6 August. Grant was aged forty-five and had a reputation within the Royal Navy as being a fine navigator, a stickler for detail and a strict disciplinarian. He was also a very sick man who was suffering from consumption, which he attempted to disguise as asthma. He had handled his earlier commands efficiently enough but had no experience of manoeuvring anything as huge as *Carmania,* which was 675 feet long and drew 44 feet of water when she was fully laden. He was, therefore, grateful for the Admiralty's permission to offer Barr the position of his adviser, with the rank of Commander, and Barr was grateful to be allowed to remain aboard what he inevitably regarded as his ship. This was a situation that would, in due course, lead to friction between the two men.

Having completed her conversion, *Carmania* sailed for Bermuda where, on the evening of 28 August, her officers held a dinner at the Bermuda Yacht Club. One of the guests was introduced as a Mr Gordon, described as the Admiralty's special representative. A gloomy individual who spoke to none of his neighbours during the meal, he subsequently depressed them. He explained that the strategic situation had changed somewhat. German activity was now centred on the southern Caribbean and South American coasts and it was affecting the important sea route from that area to the United Kingdom, along which flowed vital supplies of beef, coffee and raw materials. For that reason homeward–bound merchant ships would, for the present, follow a more southerly route after leaving the Plate and be re–routed via St Nazaire. In addition, Admiral Cradock's responsibilities had been extended to include the South American coast and as his cruisers were now working at their operational limit they would need a regular source of supplies close at hand. The same, of course, applied to the enemy's supply ships, which must be found and destroyed. For these reasons *Carmania* was to be detached from the Atlantic Patrol and was, for the moment, to act as a supply ship for Cradock's squadron and sail for Trinidad, West Indies, next morning. Understandably, the use of his fine ship in this way pushed Barr to the edge of apoplexy, but he was in no position to and kept his opinions to himself. There was, nevertheless, much in what Mr Gordon had said, for two days earlier *Dresden* had sunk the collier *Holmwood* with 6,000 toms of coal aboard.

On 2 September *Carmania* reached Trinidad, where she topped up her fuel bunkers before setting off for the mouth of the Plate two days later. The previous night had been a busy one for British intercept radio operators, listening to orders issued by the German communications centre in New York to freighters, colliers and other vessels lying in or off the South American coast, via the local embassies and consulates:

Colliers *Prussia* and *Ebenberg* to sail from Pernambuco to Trinidad [sic] and there rendezvous with armed merchant cruisers *Cap Trafalgar* and *Kronprinz Wilhelm*… .

Freighter *Corrientes* off Rio to move south to Bahia Blanca. On voyage you will be contacted by cruiser *Karlsruhe* to whom you will deliver supplies… .

Empty *Santa Lucia* and *Santa Isabel* off Trinidade to recoal at Rio Pontos and *Eleonore Wouvermans* will remain at Trinidad to resupply *Dresden*.

At this stage the British hunters were still in ignorance of their quarries' whereabouts, but on 5 September another transmission gave them their first hard evidence. Before taking *Cap Trafalgar* out on her first patrol Wirth had ordered the *Berwind* to start transferring her coal to the *Pontos* and the *Eleonore Wouvermans*. Unfortunately, some of the *Berwind's* crew had already given trouble and as the ship had been chartered by a German government agency her master considered that he was not subject to orders given by naval officers and refused to obey. *Eber* had left for Bahia Blanca some days earlier, but by using her call sign and a standard American commercial code he signalled the *Berwind's* owners in New York as follows:

> Your original instructions countermanded by local commander. Now ordered stay until *Dresden* and *Kronprinz Wilhelm* join *Cap Trafalgar* either here or Rocas. Advise which orders are acceptable. *Berwind*.

British naval intelligence was unaware that *Eber* had left German West Africa and drew the conclusion that the other named ships would joined her there or at the unidentified Rocas, having been frightened off the South American trade route by Cradock's cruisers. Did Rocas mean Rocks? Possibly. A search of the charts revealed a feature named St Paul's Rocks some 1,500 miles east-south-east of the West Indies where *Dresden* and *Karlsruhe* were known to have operated previously. Cradock was well liked in the Navy and known to be both honourable and courageous, but he was also known to be impulsive. In his view, the enemy had gathered in the area of St Paul's Rocks and thither he set off on a long wild goose chase in the cruiser *Good Hope,* to which he had transferred his flag when the *Suffolk* had failed to catch the *Karlsruhe,* leaving the cruiser screen off the South American coast dangerously thin.

Suddenly, the truth became apparent, triggered by the *Eber's* arrival off Bahia on 11 September. Her presence was noted by a member of the British Consulate and passed via Buenos Aires and Montevideo to Naval Headquarters in the West Indies. Reading *Berwind's* transmission in this light it was clear that if the gunboat had been meeting *Dresden*, *Kronprinz Wilhelm* and *Cap Trafalgar*, the rendezvous had taken place much closer than South West Africa. Therefore, *Eber* had been steaming at between 12 and 14 knots for five or six days to reach Bahia, covering a distance of approximately 1,400 miles. Taking Bahia as the centre of a drawn circle, part of the circumference passed through the Vas Rocks, not far to the east of the Islhas de los Trinidade. The result was that during the morning of 13 September, *Carmania* received orders to abandon her resupply task and inspect the Vas Rocks.

Given the number of German warships said to be in that area, Captain Grant believed that he was about to enter a hornet's nest and decided to disguise *Carmania*. He believed, incorrectly, that most German liners were equipped with three or four funnels and was obviously unaware that *Cap Trafalgar* normally carried only two. He therefore gave orders for a third funnel to be erected immediately from wood and canvas behind *Carmania's* two. As far his orders were concerned, he believed that a cautious approach from the north would enable him to inspect Vas Rocks and Trinidade from a point short of but almost between the two. This would enable the masthead lookout to report on the presence of possibly enemy shipping in the area while *Carmania* herself remained hull-down below the horizon.

At 09.30 on the morning of Monday 14 September the lookout reported that Trinidade's peak was visible. Grant altered course towards the island. At 10.00, believing that an engagement was possible within an hour or too, he followed the Royal Navy's tradition by sending the crew to an early meal. Forty-five minutes later he took the precaution of going to action stations. Grant and Barr were both studying the island intently through their binoculars. At 11.04 they both spotted three sets of masts beyond the headland. As they watched, the tallest began to move towards the open sea. A lookout post had been established at the summit of the peak and those manning it had warned Wirth of *Carmania's* approach. Deciding that she could only be an armed merchant cruiser, he decided to give battle.

Cap Trafalgar's appearance puzzled those on *Carmania's* bridge. Barr, believing that the German's two funnels were all that she had ever carried, suggested that the strange liner could well be British and possibly belonged to the Union Castle Line. Grant told his radio operator to order the stranger to identify himself and simultaneously sent *Carmania's* battle ensign soaring aloft. As the transmission remained unanswered he steered for more open sea room. Wirth, observing the change of course, swung *Cap Trafalgar* so that she was now heading directly for *Carmania,* bows on. In an event which can have few if any parallels in naval history *Carmania,* disguised as *Cap Trafalgar,* was about to engage in a duel to the death with the *Cap Trafalgar,* disguised as the *Carmania.*

At 12.15 Commander Lockyer, *Carmania's* gunnery officer, reported that the enemy was now within range. Grant ordered a shot to be fired across *Cap Trafalgar's.* The response was immediate. Up went the Imperial Navy's battle ensign and two flashes indicated that she had opened fire. Both shots went high, one passing overhead and the other bringing down her radio mast and signal halyards. A third round smashed one of her bow guns and killed most of its crew. The return salvo had devastating results. Two shells exploded in the Winter Garden, shattering acres of glass, splintering marble columns, piercing deck steam pipes and starting fires. On the bridge the quartermaster fell dead beside the wheel, while hydraulic and steam lines that provided power for the steering machinery were ruptured. The wheel itself spun wildly to port, dragging the ship off course. By main force Wirth and one of his officers managed to bring the ship back on course. By now, the foredeck and the dummy bridge that had been added as part of *Cap Trafalgar's* disguise was blazing fiercely, blinding those on the real bridge or manning the forward gun with smoke carried inboard over the bows by the wind. Wirth leaned over the bridge to shout at the forward gun crew that while they could not see the *Carmania* clearly, they should aim at her gun flashes. The order had hardly been acknowledged than a shell ricocheted off the foremast to explode against the gun shield, jamming the gun at an unusable angle, killing the gun captain and seriously wounding two of his three-man crew.

Despite this, the temporary change of course enabled Wirth's after gun to open a rapid and accurate fire on the *Carmania's* bridge, which was soon ablaze. The range had now closed sufficiently for Wirth to employ his 3.7-inch heavy machine guns. Everyone on the bridge, including the damage control party trying to extinguish the fire, dived for cover. When his rangefinder was smashed, Lockyer jumped down into the bridge, shouting to Grant that it would be a good idea to move out of machine gun range. Grant gave the order for the bridge to be abandoned and ran down the more sheltered port side of the ship to the after control position.

Barr remained a little longer to communicate with the engine room by means of the voice pipe: 'Full ahead starboard engine – full astern port!'

The ship swung to port through an arc of 90 degrees, during which the wind blew the forward off the bridge, adding to a blaze on the foredeck. Her starboard guns and after port guns promptly went into action as soon as they could bear.

'Steady!' shouted Barr. *Carmania* settled on to her new course with *Cap Trafalgar* now astern. Barr was confident that the menace of the machine guns had been reduced sufficiently and gave his final instructions: 'Full ahead all engines! Transferring to aft control!'

He then abandoned the blazing bridge to join Grant at the aft control. Grant, watching the *Cap Trafalgar*, which was making a sharp turn to starboard to follow them, commented that the German captain seemed determined to come alongside. The sheer lunacy of the idea may have raised amused grins, but the fact was that Wirth had trained a large number of his crew in boarding techniques.

While making her turn, *Carmania* had lost ground so that the distance between her and her opponent was now down to less than 1,000 yards. Lockyer saw that the moment had come to finish the business. He ran along the line of guns, ordering the crews to fire at will, aiming at the enemy's waterline. Shells began to slam into the starboard side of German hull, low down. One exploded in a coal bunker, another at the point where a bulkhead met the hull and a third penetrated a reserve bunker. The sea began to pour into the stokehold. The conventional answer was to counter-flood using the port-side tanks. Unfortunately, at that moment Wirth decided to make a sharp turn to port. The result was that the starboard side was pushed ever deeper so that even more water flooded into the hull. Frantic, an engineer officer yelled at Wirth through the voice pipe that unless he reversed the turn sharply they were finished. The captain did as he was told. This brought *Cap Trafalgar's* stern round so that it was pointing directly at *Carmania*. Wirth appreciated at once that if he did not open the range at once his ship would be battered into a wreck. As he did so, he was surprised to see that *Carmania* was also breaking off the action and heading away.

The fact was that the British ship also had urgent problems to attend to. Although no one had been aware of the passing of time, the fight had raged for an hour and a half. *Carmania's* fires were so bad that the flames had reached funnel height. Barr had been sent below to fight them with reinforced damage control parties but shell splinters had punctured water mains and hoses alike and it was no easy matter. Barr ordered the ventilators to be closed off in order to deprive the blaze of oxygen while his men struggled to beat out the blaze with stokers' shovels. At length Grant decided to renew the contest and steered towards his opponent, opening fire as soon as he was in range. Aboard *Cap Trafalgar* the situation was even worse. The raging fires below were causing the forward deck plates to glow red and the ship was making more water than could be pumped out. When *Carmania* opened fire anew Wirth changed the ship's position a point or two so that his stern gun could bear. The gunner excelled himself, firing some of the battle's best-aimed shots. In short order, the *Carmania's* aft control position was wrecked, as was the stern anchor winch. Grant hauled off until his 4.7-inch guns outranged the solitary German 4.1-inch and continued to batter the enemy ship while lines of men shouted orders to the tiller flat and engine room below.

It was soon apparent that the *Cap Trafalgar* was dying. She was stopped and beginning to list steadily to starboard. Simultaneously, the engine room warned Wirth that it was only a matter of time before the rising water reached the boilers. At this point a bizarre interruption took place. The collier *Eleonore Wouverman* suddenly interjected herself between the two ships. Aboard her was Captain Langerhannz, the *Cap*

Trafalgar's original civilian skipper. On a visit to the island's peak he had discovered an ancient Spanish mortar which he had brought down. He had restored it to working order, emplaced it on the collier's foredeck, made some propellant out of black powder fog maroons and manufactured an assortment of missiles from scrap metal. Now he felt the moment had come to go to the assistance of his former command. He fired the mortar, but apart from dense powder smoke that hid the entire scene, does not appear to have done any damage. The collier then moved into the lee of the *Cap Trafalgar* while he struggled to reload.

Casualties were beginning to mount aboard the stationary German liner. A shell burst against the ship's superstructure, driving a jagged fragment of bridge rail into Wirth's left armpit. Recovering slightly, he gave the order for the crew to abandon ship, specifying that no officer should do so until the last man had gone. Many of the boats had been smashed but enough were lowered to accommodate most of the survivors, although some were forced to swim. The officers assembled on the bridge then, as the ship lay on her starboard side, walked down it into the water, assisting those who were wounded. The bow was now under water but suddenly the ship lurched and for a moment she returned to an even keel, then her stern lifted and she slid beneath the surface, gathering speed as she did so. Sharks added an horrific element to the scene, taking some of the swimmers before turning on each other in a feeding frenzy. The *Eleonore Wouvermans* did not fire her mortar again and concentrated on taking survivors aboard. Wirth was not among them, the effects of his wound and the effort of swimming having resulted in a fatal heart attack. In total, fifteen member of the *Cap Trafalgar's* lost their lives as a result of the action, five were seriously wounded and another sixty-one received less serious injuries.

It was about this time that Barr shouted something to Grant. Just what has never been recorded officially and although Barr made a brief reference to it in later life, the precise meaning of what he wrote is far from clear. His tone, however, was sharp enough for those around to stop what they were doing and look at the two senior officers. Was he suggesting that as the collier was now fully engaged in picking up survivors the *Carmania* should cease firing on her? In fact, the gun crews ceased firing of their own accord. Or was it in his mind that if she remained on an upwind heading the fire would gut her long before it could be brought under control? Probably the latter as Grant gave the order to go about, commenting to Barr in a normal conversational tone that they should now concentrate on getting the fire out. It would certainly have been to the fore of Barr's mind that his own well-loved ship had taken more than enough punishment and the time had come to end it. She had sustained no less than seventy-nine major hits, which was remarkable considering that *Cap Trafalgar* only mounted two guns. Her casualties amounted to nine killed and twenty-six seriously wounded.

By dusk, the blaze was under control but she still lacked engine room and steering controls while her boats and all her deck machinery had been shot to pieces. Her crew, however, did manage to activate a spare radio and rig a jury antenna and in response to her signals the cruiser *Bristol* arrived, sending an engineering party aboard to assist with temporary repairs. In the meantime the *Eleonore Wouvermans* was allowed to leave the area unmolested, on passage to Buonas Aires where those aboard were interned. *Bristol* then escorted the *Carmania* to Abrolhos Rocks where she handed over her charge to *Cornwall*. After further repairs the two sailed in convoy to Gibraltar where *Carmania* was returned to duty after eight weeks' intensive work.

It was some time before the crew knew the identity of the ship they had sunk. Grant asked the Admiralty to pay prize money and on 27 March 1916 the High Court granted the sum of £2,115 for distribution. Grant had already taken up a post ashore and was created a Commander of the Bath. All but two of his officers received a Mention in Despatches. Barr also received the CB but because of ill health he was declared unfit for sea duty with the Royal Navy and returned to the Merchant service, becoming Cunard's Senior Commodore. Lockyer was awarded the Distinguished Service Order and returned to retired life shortly after the action.

Carmania resumed her patrols on completion of the repairs, her beat being the Portuguese coast and the Atlantic islands. In 1916 she played a part in the Gallipoli campaign and thereafter was used as a troop ship. When the war ended she conveyed Canadian troops homeward. She became a passenger liner once more in 1920 and was honoured by the Navy League with a silver plate that had once graced Lord Nelson's table aboard the *Victory,* one of a set bought by the League for presentation to ships that had distinguished themselves during the war. *Carmania* was the only civilian ship to be honoured in this way. After refitting in 1923 she continued her long and eventful career for a further nine years before being scrapped.

CHAPTER 4

Pacific Odyssey

In August 1914 Germany's Far Eastern and Pacific possessions included the Marshall Islands, the northern part of New Guinea, the Solomon Islands and the Bismarck Archipelago, the Palau, Marianna and Caroline Islands, and the Samoan islands of Upola and Savii. The jewel in Germany's Far Eastern crown, however, was Kiachow Bay and the surrounding territories in the northern Chinese province of Shantung, leasing from the Chinese government in 1898 for a period of ninety-nine years. A city named Tsingtao was built on the tip of the peninsula separating the bay from the Yellow Sea, specifically designed to enhance German prestige in the area. No expense was spared in laying out its boulevards, public buildings and gardens. In addition, there were restaurants and hotels to rival any in the Orient, plus a temperate climate and sandy beaches. The Germans were proud of their investment, naming Tsingtao the Riviera of the Far East. To protect their investment, they fortified the landward approaches to the city and stationed a naval squadron in the harbour.

Put at its simplest, Tsingtao was a part of Kaiser Wilhelm's plan to project Imperial Germany as a global power with a navy that could challenge that of Great Britain. Unfortunately, that particular part of the plan fell apart in 1902 when neighbouring Japan concluded an alliance with the United Kingdom, relations between the two countries having become close as a result of the Royal Navy's having overseen the development and training of the Imperial Japanese Navy. It was felt that in the event of a war between Great Britain and Germany, Japan would certainly honour her alliance. The reality was that the Japanese wanted Tsingtao and at that period of history if they wanted something they usually got it by one means or another. Far from being a fortress, Tsingtao had become a trap. German worries on that score were briefly relieved by the Russo-Japanese War of 1904–5, but returned ten-fold when Japan emerged the victor, having humbled the apparent might of Russia with comparative ease.

At the beginning of August 1914 the major German naval presence at Tsingtao was Vice Admiral Count Maximilian von Spee's East Asia Squadron. At full strength it consisted of the armoured cruisers *Scharnhorst* (flag, Captain Schultz) and *Gneisenau* (Captain Maerker), armed with eight 8.2-inch and six 5.9-inch guns, and the light cruisers *Emden* (Captain von Müller), *Nurnberg* (Captain von Schonberg) and *Leipzig* (Captain Haun) armed with ten 4.1-inch guns, although *Leipzig* had been temporarily detached to protect German interests along the west coast of Mexico. Also present at Tsingtao were an elderly destroyer, *S90*, and a number of gunboats that could be used to convert civilian liners into armed merchant cruisers, and an Austrian light cruiser, the *Kaiserin Elizabeth,* which was paying a courtesy call. Elsewhere, a few more gunboats were operating on China's rivers or based at Shanghai.

Of these, *Scharnhorst* and *Gneisenau* were obviously the most formidable, being considered two of the best gunnery ships in the entire Imperial Navy; *Gneisenau*, in fact, had won the Kaiser's Gold Cup for Gunnery and her sister was not far behind. This was most important as Spee was well aware that his squadron would not survive an encounter with the Japanese fleet. Nor could it hope to remain for long at any of Germany's Pacific colonies which were incapable of either supplying the squadron with the necessary technical and logistic support, or defending themselves. He was well aware of Japanese ambitions regarding Tsingtao and conscious that in the event of a war with Great Britain she would activate these very quickly. The squadron's only remaining alternative, therefore, was to head for home by crossing the Pacific, rounding Cape Horn and then possibly sailing north up the less frequented sea lanes of the Atlantic. Supply ships and colliers had been engaged to accompany the squadron and the considerable German community resident in South America was instructed to provide further support as required. It was a desperately risky undertaking, but *Scharnhorst* and *Gneisenau* would provide the squadron with a slim chance of success as the only opposition likely to be encountered, in the early stages of the voyage at least, were slower British cruisers that were out-ranged and out-gunned. Any battle would be fought at a range of Spee's choosing, a range at which the British could do little or no damage.

On 1 August Germany declared war on Russia. Three days later the East Asia Squadron scored its first success. While cruising off the Korean port of Pusan, Captain von Müller's *Emden* intercepted the small Russian liner *Ryazan* which, while owned by the Russian Volunteer Fleet Association, was still engaged in her peacetime role of conveying civilian passengers. At first, her British captain tried to run for it, a futile exercise considering that her maximum speed was only 14 knots. This ended when he recognised his pursuer was the *Emden* and, out of consideration for the women and children aboard, he surrendered. Müller escorted her into Tsingtao where she was armed with eight 4.1-inch guns inherited from the ancient gunboat *Kormoran*, whose name she adopted. Simultaneously, another liner, the Norddeutscher Lloyd Steamship Line's *Prinz Eitel Friedrich*, named after the Kaiser's second son, was being converted to the role of armed merchant cruiser by the addition of two 4.1-inch and four 3.4-inch guns inherited from the gunboats *Tiger* and *Luchs* (Lynx). The crew was also provided by the two gunboats. *Prinz Eitel Friedrich* was to form part of the East Asia Squadron under Lieutenant Commander Thierichens, formerly of the *Luchs*. *Emden* and these two recent additions to the German naval strength were to leave Tsingtao as soon as the work of conversion had been completed and join the rest of the squadron at sea.

On 15 August the Japanese gave Germany an ultimatum, demanding that she withdraw all her warships from Far Eastern waters and surrender Tsingtao and the entire leased territory of Kiaochow 'without condition or compensation'. Obviously, no self-respecting government would comply with such demands and these, as expected, were ignored. The Japanese had been forming a military and naval task force to attack Tsingtao for some time and on 23 August formally declared war on Germany. Four days later a blockading force arrived off the port. This was followed shortly after by the besieging force, which included a small British contingent. This was received politely but left in no doubt that this was Japanese business being conducted for the sole benefit of Japan. In the event, the German garrison held out, with no hope of relief, until 7 November. By then, Spee and his ships were half a world away and their crews were celebrating a victory.

At the end of June Spee had taken the *Scharnhorst* and *Gneisenau* on a protracted cruise of the central Pacific. On 6 August he reached Ponape in the Marshall Islands, joining *Nurnberg* which had only just been relieved by *Leipzig* off the Mexican coast. He headed for Pagan in the Marianas group, some 1,000 miles to the north where on 12 August he was joined by the *Emden, Prinz Eitel Freidrich* and *Kormoran*, plus four supply vessels from Tsingtao. Four more supply ships had been sunk or captured by Vice Admiral Sir Martin Jerram's China Squadron, and while these could be replaced by German embassies and consulates elsewhere, it was a sharp reminder that the Imperial German Navy had very few friends in the Pacific, for to the south Rear Admiral Sir George Patey's squadron of the Royal Australian Navy barred any progress while to the north the Japanese were on the point of declaring war. On 13 August Spee held a Captains' conference aboard his flagship indicating his intention to proceed in a generally south-eastern direction towards Chile. Müller expressed reservations about the difficulty of coaling so many ships and the absence of enemy shipping lanes along the route, and expressed the view that a single light cruiser operating in the Indian Ocean could cause considerable damage and tie down British resources across a wide area. Spee agreed and gave the task to Müller, whose *Emden* was the fastest of the squadron's light cruisers. The admiral left for Eniwetok Atoll with the rest of the squadron later in the day, while the following morning *Emden*, accompanied by the collier *Markomannia*, set out on a cruise that would make her one of the most famous German warships of the war.

At Eniwetok the East Asia Squadron spent three days coaling in the broad lagoon. *Prinz Eitel Friedrich* and *Kormoran* were detached to raid shipping routes in Australian waters and on 22 August *Nurnberg* was sent to Honolulu from where a signal could be despatched informing the Admiralty in Berlin that Spee was heading for Chile and expected to arrive at Juan Fernandez on 15 October. It was requested that coal supplies be sent there from San Francisco and Valparaiso.

On 26 August the squadron coaled in the lagoon of Majuro Atoll, where a signal was received informing Spee of Japan's declaration of war. The Allies, on the other hand, had no idea of Spee's whereabouts. The East Asia Squadron had apparently vanished into thin air and no amount of searching could detect a hint of its presence. Having left Majuro, Spee headed due east for Christmas Island which was reached on 7 September. *Nurnberg* rejoined shortly after, having called at Fanning Island and cut the cable connecting Honolulu with Fiji. She brought with her the news that troops belonging to the New Zealand Army had occupied German Samoa. Spee believed that the invaders' troop transports and supply ships could well still be present in the area, but when he approached the town of Apia at first light on 14 September the only vessel present was a small sailing ship which certainly did not justify the expenditure of ammunition that could not be replaced.

The squadron resumed its eastwards course, calling at Suvorov Island, then Bora Bora in the Society Islands, then the French island of Tahiti at dawn on 22 September. Here, thanks to thorough preparations on the part of the Governor, the garrison was wide awake and alert. *Scharnhorst* and *Gneisenau* became involved in duel with the fort and a French gunboat, the *Zelée*, which turned out to be fruitless as all pilotage marks had been removed from the entrance to the harbour. As a result, the Germans had to watch helplessly while the Governor blew up the port's warehouses and set fire to his coal stocks. Annoyed by the pointless expenditure of ammunition, Spee resumed his eastwards voyage, pausing at the Marquesas Islands to coal and re-provision from 26 September to 3 October. Meanwhile, the Governor of Tahiti had sent warning of the squadron's presence to Samoa and in due course the news reached the Admiralty in London. For no intelligible reason the latter believed that Spee was actually heading *west* and told Patey to base himself at Suva in the Fijian Islands. Simultaneously, Spee was informing Berlin that he was now heading for Valparaiso via Easter Island and Juan Fernandez, to which places the German Consul in San Francisco was to despatch coal. In addition, the signals office aboard the flagship was able to listen to radio traffic between the *Leipzig* and the *Dresden*, confirming that both light cruisers were still active off the west coast of South America. Thus, when the East Asia Squadron reached Easter Island on 12 October, Spee was able to plan the concentration of all German naval units in the area.

When war began to seem inevitable, Captain Haun sailed *Leipzig* north from her station off the Mexican coast to a point near the entrance to San Francisco harbour, where he hoped to prey on Allied shipping. However, following instructions from the Admiralty, British shipping remained snug inside the bay. There were, however, rumours that two enemy cruisers, the British *Newcastle* and the Japanese *Idzumo* were heading for the area and Haun began to look for prey further south. On 27 August, while off the coast of Lower California, he received a signal from Berlin instructing him to operate off South America and, possibly, in the Atlantic. On 11 September he had his first success, sinking the steamer *Elsinore,* on passage in ballast to Panama. A week later *Leipzig* reached the Galapagos Islands. On 25 September she sank the freighter *Bankfield*, on passage from Panama to the United Kingdom with cargo of sugar. After that, there was no further contact with Allied merchant shipping but on 1 October he received orders from Berlin to cooperate with *Dresden*. For the moment he had no contact with the latter but, by coincidence, a shortage of coal induced him to head for Easter Island. On the night of 2/3 October *Dresden* did manage to get through by radio and informed him that she, too, was heading for Easter Island.

Dresden had rounded the Horn on 18 September and immediately become involved in an incident that was to have far-reaching consequences. She had not long emerged from the Straits of Magellan when she encountered the Royal Mail Ship *Ortega*, travelling in the opposite direction. *Ortega*, under the command of Captain Douglas Kinnier, was on passage from Valparaiso to Montevideo by way of the passage. She had aboard cargo valued at £117,000, Admiralty mail with a secure classification and 300 French reservists heading for home to rejoin the Army. Kinnier was aware that the odds were stacked against him for *Ortega* was only capable of a maximum speed on 14 knots while, inevitably, that of the German cruiser was much greater. Whatever happened, he was determined to give the enemy a run for his money.

Aboard *Dresden*, Captain Ludecke ordered a round to be fired across *Ortega's* bows as a signal that she should heave to. Kinnier ignored it but swung away on a course that would take him to Cape George. Made aware of the situation, the engine room staff decided to ignore the manufacturer's recommendations and thrashed the ship into a hitherto unheard of rivet-rattling 18 knots. *Dresden* had not the slightest difficulty in keeping up and now opened fire in earnest but to little effect as *Ortega* was stern-on and presented only a small, narrow target.

Despite shells sending up fountains of water nearby, Kinnier was not giving up. His plan was to take *Ortega* into uncharted shallow waters in which *Dresden* could not follow. He steered the ship into the little-used Nelson's Strait, letting her speed fall away as boats were lowered. For almost 100 miles of narrow, tortuous channel the boats took frequent soundings while *Ortega* followed slowly behind. Ludecke probably thought Kinnier was mad to hazard his ship in this way and quickly abandoned the chase. At length, Kinnier brought *Ortega* out into the Straits of Magellan and then completed the passage into the Atlantic by way of Smyth's Channel. On reaching Rio de Janeiro to report the incident, he expressed himself quietly satisfied that neither the enemy nor nature had succeeded in putting a scratch on his plates.

Having coaled at Easter Island and obtained fresh supplies of meat, the assembled German squadron sailed for Mas a Fuera, an isolated rock that provided a protected anchorage, another 1,500 miles to the east, arriving on 26 October. Here, to everyone's surprise, it was joined by the armed merchant cruiser *Prinz Eitel Friedrich*, which had been forced to abandon her abortive cruise in Australian waters for lack of fuel supplies. The same was true of the *Kormoron*, which after searching for Allied shipping had only sufficient fuel left to reach the American island of Guam, where she was interned. There her crew enjoyed a restful war until the United States declared war on Germany, becoming prisoners of war after scuttling their ship on 7 April 1917.

Ortega's experience had convinced Cradock that the reinforced East Asia Squadron was somewhere west of South America, but not as far west as the Admiralty seemed to think. There was also a suspicion that *Karlsruhe* was still active somewhere in the Atlantic. Therefore, while Cradock began to operate round the Horn from Port Stanley in the Falkland Islands, several more cruisers under Rear Admiral Stoddart remained active on the east coast to protect the vital shipping lanes to the United Kingdom. During the next few weeks the Admiralty's faulty intelligence and poor appreciation of the situation involved Cradock and his ships, including the ~~protected~~ armored cruisers *Monmouth* and *Good Hope*, the light cruiser *Glasgow* and the armed merchant cruiser *Otranto*, on a number of fruitless patrols in atrocious weather, demonstrating the futility of senior officers attempting to control actions from which they were thousands of miles distant. They also beefed up Cradock's squadron with the 1899 battleship *Canopus* under Captain H.S. Grant. *Canopus* was armed with four 12-inch and twelve 6-inch guns and therefore had plenty of punch, had she been allowed to use it. The problem was that with a maximum speed of 12 knots she would not as her likely German opponents were much faster and could keep her at arm's length.

Cradock was well-liked throughout the Royal Navy. He had previously seen active service in Egypt and the Sudan, and in China during the Boxer Rebellion, storming the formidable Taku Forts at the entrance to the Pei-ho River in a joint Anglo-German operation. One of the German officers present on this occasion was his present opponent, Maximilian von Spee, with whom he was personally acquainted. An amiable man, he was good company and while he had never married he enjoyed the company of women. His closest companion was his dog, which accompanied him whether he was ashore or afloat. While his home was his cabin, he had few personal possessions, the exception being a cloisonné vase that he had acquired in China. A keen huntsman, he was known to comment that if he did not meet his death in action he would prefer it to take place in the hunting field.

Spee had served in the Imperial Navy for thirty-seven years. A happily married man whose two sons were serving in his squadron, he was the opposite of the British cartoon version of a German senior officer, being noted for the courtesy and good manners with which he conducted his business. Professionally, he was a gunnery expert with additional experience in weapon development. His recognition of the need for thorough training had brought his squadron's gunnery to the highest possible standard. He had seen active service in the Cameroons and China where his natural aggression first became apparent.

The circumstances that brought these two men and their squadrons together were curiously similar. *Glasgow* had called at Valparaiso and Spee saw an opportunity to destroy her. Likewise, Cradock was hunting a German light cruiser that had been reported in the area. During the afternoon of 1 November the two squadrons were converging on each other off Coronel, the Germans from the north and the British from the south. Cradock, having decided to leave the battleship *Canopus* behind to escort two colliers, possessed the *Good Hope*, *Monmouth*, *Glasgow* and the armed merchant cruiser *Otranto*. Spee had *Scharnhorst*, *Gneisenau* and *Leipzig* immediately available, but *Nurnberg* and *Dresden*, some distance to the north, were ordered to join immediately. Likewise, each squadron having sighted the other's smoke, Cradock swung his line east towards the enemy, then south. By 18.00 the opposing squadrons were running on approximately parallel lines.

Many have questioned why Cradock chose to force a battle on Spee when he had a seriously inferior force. For a few moments he had a slight tactical advantage in that the setting sun illuminated the German ships and blinded their gunners. Then, the sun set, leaving the British ships silhouetted against its afterglow. Their opponents, however, were difficult to spot against the dark background of the land to the east. Unfortunately, Cradock considered himself to be a prisoner of tradition. Ever since the days of Sir Richard Grenville the Royal Navy had never shirked a fight against odds and rather than surrender many of its ships had preferred to go down with their colours flying than surrender. The latter had never been considered mandatory and it was considered to be no disgrace for a captain to surrender his ship provided that she no longer possessed the means to fight.

At 17.00, with a heavy sea running and the range at 12,300 yards, Spee ordered his ships to open fire. *Good Hope's* 9.2-inch gun was put out of action by *Scharnhorst's* third salvo, while a shell from *Gneisenau* blew the roof off *Monmouth's* forward 6-inch turret. A heavy internal explosion then blew the wreckage of the turret itself overboard and started a blaze on the forecastle. *Leipzig* and *Glasgow* were also firing at each other, but the former's guns were not yet within range while it was difficult for the latter to spot her own fall of shot. *Otranto*, unable to contribute to the battle, pulled out of the British line to starboard.

By 19.10 the outcome of the battle was no longer in doubt although fighting continued. For a while, *Good Hope's* one remaining 9.2-inch was the only British gun capable of reaching the enemy, but Cradock doggedly closed the range between the opposing ships. By 19.35 this was down to 5,500 yards, enabling *Good Hope* and *Monmouth* to make some reply with their 6-inch guns. It was of little use, being a contest between reservists who had been allowed only four practice rounds per gun with which to retrain after being recalled to the service, and the finest gunners in the Imperial German Navy. Both ships had been subjected an unending rain of shells. At 19.57 *Good Hope* was blown apart by an explosion that sent flames roaring to a height of 200 feet; at 20.00 the shattered hull went down, taking all aboard with it.

By 20.15 *Monmouth* was down by the bows, making serious quantities of water, listing to port and with an internal fire glowing through her after portholes. *Glasgow* had seemed to bear a charmed life in the face of the combined enemy fire but there was nothing she could do for the stricken *Monmouth* and, realising the importance of reporting what had taken place, she escaped into the western darkness. She did not realise it, but she was pursued for a while by the *Nurnberg* and *Dresden*.

At about 21.00 Captain von Schonberg put *Nurnberg* on a west-south-westerly course towards distant column of smoke rising skywards on the port bow. As the origin of the smoke came into view he snapped on a searchlight revealing *Monmouth,* badly battered and listing heavily to port but still moving slowly and with her White Ensign still flying. Schonberg opened fire at 1,000 yards range, closing to 600 yards. Because of *Monmouth's* list her port guns were actually pointing at the water and clearly incapable of returning fire. Schonberg ceased firing, not wishing to further inflict death or injury on a defenceless enemy. However, *Monmouth* was seen to be turning slowly towards *Nurnberg* as though to ram or engage with her starboard guns and across the water her officers could be heard shouting for men from the damage control parties to assist in manning the latter. In addition, her White Ensign was still flying defiantly and obvious that whoever was commanding her had no intention of surrendering. *Nurnberg* therefore opened fire again, punching shells into the unprotected parts of *Monmouth's* hull. Her list grew ever greater so that her starboard guns were pointing skywards and finally she capsized and went to the bottom with her colours still flying. The rescue of survivors would have been attempted had it been possible to launch boats in the heavy seas running, but it was not; furthermore, in the cold heaving waters a man's life could be measured in minutes.

Although *Glasgow* and *Otranto* escaped to fight another day, the Battle of Coronel was the Royal Navy's first major defeat for a century. Admiral Cradock and over 1,500 of his men had lost their lives and two cruisers had been sunk. Victory, goes the saying, has many fathers, but defeat is an orphan. The Admiralty and Cradock himself both share a degree of responsibility for what had happened, but the truth went much deeper than that. The continuous advance of technology had ensured that naval warfare had changed beyond recognition. No longer was it a matter of laying alongside an enemy and pounding away until he surrendered. The side with the most powerful long-range guns, the stoutest armour, the greatest speed and the most thorough training would, given approximate parity in other areas, always emerge the victor. In contrast to the disaster that had overtaken Cradock's squadron, Spee's ships had sustained just five hits that had inflicted minimal damage, thanks to the poor quality of the British shells. Personnel casualties in the East Asia Squadron amounted to three men slightly wounded.

After the battle Spee took *Scharnhorst*, *Gneisenau* and *Nurnberg* into Valparaiso, while *Leipzig* and *Dresden* were sent to Mas a Fuera. This reflected the application of the neutrality laws which permitted only three warships of a belligerent power to be present in a neutral harbour at any one time, and Spee's choice suggests that he was rewarding the crews of those ships that had played the most significant part in the battle with a run ashore. The city's German community was overjoyed by their victory and gave them a hero's welcome. The German ambassador to Chile, a Herr von Erckherdt, provided Spee with mixed news. On the one hand, he believed that he could guarantee the East Asia Squadron's coal supply; on the other, intelligence had been received that two Japanese cruisers were heading for American waters. During the next few days the ambassador also passed on to Spee a series of signals received from Berlin. The general tone was that he should try to break through and reach home and at one stage it was suggested that the High Seas Fleet might render assistance. Spee not only knew that this was optimistic nonsense, but was aware that the number of alternatives open to him was shrinking rapidly. He could not retrace his steps across the Pacific, nor could he take a northerly route to the Panama Canal because of the continued concentration of Allied warships in the area. That left only the Atlantic route, which would involve rounding the Horn, and nothing was more certain than that following its defeat at Coronel the Royal Navy would send reinforcement into the South Atlantic. If that happened, he was in no condition to fight a prolonged action as Coronel had left *Scharnhorst* and *Gneisenau* with just 50 per cent of their ammunition while his light cruisers were slightly better off with 60 per cent. As Geoffrey Bennett recounts in his book *Coronel and the Falklands*, he was able to unburden himself to an old acquaintance, a retired German Navy doctor who had made his home in Valparaiso:

'I am quite homeless. I cannot reach Germany; we possess no other secure harbour; I must plough the seas of the world doing as much mischief as I can, till my ammunition is exhausted, or till a foe far superior in power succeeds in catching me.' Forced to spend some time in the German Club he was irritated by a rowdy civilian who proposed the toast 'Damnation to the British Navy.' Having seen that Navy fight and die when confronted by hopeless odds he replied coldly, 'I drink to the memory of a gallant and honourable foe.'

Shortly after he left Valparaiso to join *Dresden* and *Leipzig* at Mas a Fuera. While there he made up his mind to round the Horn into the Atlantic but sent them on a brief visit to Valparaiso to scotch a current rumour that they had been sunk at Coronel. In fact the interpretation placed on their visit by British intelligence was that the entire East Asia Squadron was still somewhere off the Chilean coast. On 15 November *Scharnhorst*, *Gneisenau* and *Nurnberg* began moving south, accompanied by two supply ships, the *Baden* and the *Santa Isabella*. *Dresden* and *Leipzig* rejoined on three days later, having a captured and sunk the 3,600-ton freighter *North Wales* on 16 November. For the moment *Prinz Eitel Friedrich* would remain in the general area, transmitting a string of dummy signals that might suggest to the Japanese to the north that Spee's ships were still in the area.

On 21 November the squadron halted for several days in St Quentin Bay where Spee received a signal to the effect that the Kaiser had honoured him with the Iron Cross First and Second Class while 300 Iron Crosses were to be distributed to the squadron's officers and men as appropriate. After coaling from three Chilean colliers that were operating illegally, the squadron possessed sufficient fuel to last well up the east coast of South America. Almost four weeks after Coronel, Spee set out for the Horn, little realising that his delay in doing so was the first of two fatal mistakes that would destroy his command.

The battle cruiser *Goeben*, flagship of Germany's Mediterranean Squadron, was well armed and faster than her likely British opponents. After her escape to Constantinople she was transferred to the Turkish Navy, of which she became flagship, changing her name to *Yavuz Sultan Selim*. She saw extensive service against the Russians in the Black Sea and was retained by the Turkish Navy after the First World War. In 1936 she was renamed *Yavuz*. She was finally scrapped in 1973, the last of Kaiser Wilhelm II's High Seas Fleet. *Picture credit: US Navy*

The light cruiser *Breslau*. The volume of smoke clearly indicates the quantity of coal required to maintain this speed. In Turkish service she was renamed *Medili*.

A blurred but historically interesting snapshot taken from the *Goeben*'s stern. Great Britain and Germany are still some hours away from war. Two British battle cruisers, *Indefatigable* and *Indomitable*, have just passed *Goeben* and *Breslau* on an opposite course which they are now reversing so as to position themselves on the *Goeben*'s port and starboard quarters. When the time came, this would have enabled them to engage *Goeben* from different angles while the German ship would have to split her fire in reply. In the event, *Goeben*'s speed enabled her to pull out of range and then out of sight. The intense effort claimed the lives of several stokers from heatstroke.

Modern and fast, *Karlsruhe* easily outran Admiral Christopher Cradock's ships in the West Indies, causing him to transfer his flag to the cruiser *Good Hope* with consequences that were later to prove disastrous. *Karlsruhe* wreaked havoc among British merchant shipping before she was blown apart by an internal explosion, the reason for which has never been fully established.

'The deeds of the *Karlsruhe*' reads this German memorial postcard, published after her loss. In fact, this particular type of patriotic publication did more harm than good. German cruiser captains of the period made considerable efforts to ensure the survival of their victims' crews, arranging for them to be landed in neutral ports. The suggestion given to enemy and neutral nations in this case was that once ships had been sunk, their crews and passengers were left to their fate, which was simply not true.

The Islhas de los Trinidade, 400 miles off the Brazilian coast, were the scene of a ferocious duel between armed merchant cruisers respectively the British *Carmania* and the German *Cap Trafalgar*. The latter was sunk but *Carmania* was seriously damaged that she requir[ed] a long period in dock before returning to duty. One curious feature of the engagement was tha[t] the *Cap Trafalgar* had disguised herself as the *Carmania* by removing her third funnel.

The armoured cruisers *Scharnhorst* and *Gneisenau* were armed with eight 8.2-inch, six 5.9-inch and eighteen 3.4-inch guns apiece and outgunned all of Admiral Cradock's ships with the exception of the battleship *Canopus*, which he chose to leave behind because of her low speed. In addition, the standard of gunnery in both German ships was exceptionally high. *Scharnhorst* was the flagship of Vice Admiral Graf von Spee.

The lines of the light cruiser *Leipzig* give her a slightly old-fashioned look although she was only a little older than the other light cruisers in the East Asia Squadron and carried the same basic armament of ten 4.1-inch guns. She was, however, somewhat slower.

Nurnberg was not present at the beginning of the Battle of Coronel but came across the crippled *Monmouth* in the dusk and sank her when she refused to surrender.

The two 9.2-inch guns of Admiral Cradock's flagship, the armoured cruiser *Good Hope*, were the only weapons in the British squadron capable of inflicting serious damage on the *Scharnhorst* and *Gneisenau*. One was destroyed at the beginning of the action and the second was overwhelmed by the weight and accuracy of the German fire.

The armoured cruiser *Monmouth* survived the opening phase of the battle but was so seriously damaged that she was unable to return the *Nurnberg*'s fire in a later encounter and, like the *Good Hope*, was sunk with the loss of all hands.

The 12-inch guns of the battleship *Canopus*, serving as Guardship South Atlantic in 1914, fired the first shots in the Battle of the Falkland Islands but for some reason her crew were not granted a share in the prize money awarded by the Admiralty.

The battle cruiser *Invincible* working up to her maximum speed as she pursues Spee's East Asia Squadron.

A magazine artist's portrayal of the opening stages of the Battle of the Falkland Islands. From left to right the ships shown are the cruisers *Glasgow* and *Kent*, the battle cruisers *Invincible* and *Inflexible*, the armoured cruisers *Scharnhorst* and *Gneisenau*, and the light cruisers *Nurnberg*, *Leipzig* and *Dresden. Picture credit: Mary Evans Picture Library*

The last moments of the *Scharnhorst*. The nearest ship was the *Invincible* but with the battle still raging it was impossible for her to engage in rescue work and there were no survivors.

The *Gneisenau* sank shortly after. As there were no enemy ships remaining in the area, *Inflexible* was able to launch her boats and pick up the few survivors.

Spee had attempted to escape to the south-east with his heavy units and so give his light cruisers a chance to escape to the south. The ruse did not work and a series of duels developed. Here, *Kent* is shown sinking *Nurnberg*. *Picture credit: Mary Evans Picture Library*

Glasgow and *Cornwall* sinking *Leipzig* while *Dresden* escapes to the west. *Picture credit: Mary Evans Picture Library*

Having escaped the destruction of the East Asia Squadron at the Battle of the Falkland Islands, the *Dresden* remained at large until 14 March 1915, when she was finally cornered by the British cruisers *Kent* and *Glasgow* at Mas a Fuera (better known as Robinson Crusoe Island) in the Juan Fernandez Group. This romanticised painting shows the subsequent engagement taking place at a much closer range than was actually the case.

Dresden had all but expended her supplies of coal and ammunition and fought for only three minutes before hoisting white flag on her foremast. After scuttling charges had been placed the crew went ashore and were interned in what was neutral Chilean territory. Having spent so long in Caribbean and South American waters, many of her crew chose not to return to Germany when the war ended.

A morale-raising postcard issued in Germany showing the *Emden* and her captain. The caption reads: 'The Iron Cross [awarded to] the heroic *Emden*.'

The Russian cruiser *Zemchug*, sunk by the *Emden* in Penang harbour. Discipline aboard this ship left much to be desired.

Another of *Emden*'s victims at Penang was the French destroyer *Mousquet*, which was only sunk after a very gallant fight.

HMAS *Sydney* finally cornered *Emden* in the Cocos Islands. She out-gunned her opponent and the outcome of the duel was never in doubt.

Australians examine the battered wreck of the *Emden*, run aground to prevent her sinking. Little did they realise that *Emden*'s landing party, after many adventures, would actually succeed in reaching Germany by way of the Turkish Empire.

HMS *Pegasus*, launched in 1898, is seen here in her Victorian livery of white hull and buff funnels. When *Konigsberg* discovered her in Zanzibar harbour her boilers were being cleaned and her guns were outranged by the German cruiser. She was, therefore, a sitting target and was sunk without being able to offer serious resistance.

The shallow-draft monitor *Mersey* and her sister ship *Severn* were armed with three 6-inch guns and two 4.7-inch howitzers apiece. Their fire was controlled by aircraft that signalled corrections by radio back to the ships and ultimately damaged *Konigsberg* so badly that she had to be scuttled. *Picture credit: Imperial War Museum Neg No SP84*

The wreck of the *Konigsberg*. Despite her destruction, her 4.1-inch guns were landed and most were fitted with field carriages in railway workshops at Dar es Salaam and employed in support of German troops during the East African campaign.

The *Graf von Gotzen* in 1916, flying the Imperial German Navy's ensign. One of the Konigsberg's 4.1-inch guns has been mounted on her forecastle. Built in 1913 by the Meyer Werft shipyard in northern Germany, she was shipped out to East Africa in sections and assembled on the shores of Lake Tanganyika. Raised after being scuttled to prevent her capture by the British, she continued in commercial service until 2010, when she was finally retired after nearly a century of service.

Gunnery drill aboard the *Graf von Gotzen*. Apart from some naval caps and a few tunics borrowed from the army, the German flotilla on Lake Tanganyika seems to have been relaxed in its concept of uniforms.

Mimi and *Toutou* were launched with railway assistance after their long journey from Cape Town. Spicer-Simson, wearing his skirt, is the closest to the camera of the naval personnel. *Picture credit: Imperial War Museum Neg No Q 67680*

The two British gunboats fitting out shortly before their engagement with the German *Kigani*.
Picture credit: Imperial War Museum Neg No Q 67687

Her tall masts and multiple ventilators easily identified the protected cruiser *Highflyer*. Her armament consisted of eleven 6-inch and nine 12-pounder guns. On 26 August 1914 she came across the German liner *Kaiser Wilhelm der Grosse*, recently converted to the role of commerce raider, coaling in the Spanish waters of Rio de Oro.

When *Highflyer* opened fire the German colliers scattered for safety but *Kaiser Wilhelm der Grosse* replied at once and, despite being hit repeatedly, put up a stiff fight. *Highflyer* can just be made out on the horizon on the extreme left of the picture.

Battered by 6-inch shells and ablaze aft, the raider was clearly doomed and rolled over onto her port side. Some of her crew can be seen heading for the shore in their boats.

On 10 March 1917 the raider *Möwe* came across the New Zealand Shipping Company's freighter *Otaki*. Despite being hopelessly out-gunned, the latter's captain decided to make a fight of it with the raider, upon which he inflicted near-fatal damage before his own ship was finally sunk. Chivalrously, although the *Möwe* was in danger of sinking herself, she picked up the *Otaki's* survivors.

The Japanese loner *Hitachi Maru* was run down by the raider *Wolf* off the southern end of the Maldive Islands on 26 September 1917. She refused to stop until forced to surrender after fourteen of her crew had been killed and six wounded. Although some of her crew were seen moving around the liner's stern gun there is some doubt that it actually opened fire. *Wolf's* scout plane *Wolfchen* (Little Wolf) can be seen over-flying the interception.

CHAPTER 5

Death in Southern Seas

While the population of Germany rejoiced at Spee's victory off Coronel, regarding it as revenge for the humiliation of the High Seas Fleet in the Heligoland Bight some months earlier, in the United Kingdom the shock engendered by the defeat was made all the sharper by the recent, albeit none too successful, bombardment of Yarmouth on the East Anglian coast. Public and press alike formed an opinion that something was seriously amiss at the Admiralty and such was the vitriolic nature of criticism that the First Sea Lord, Admiral Prince Louis of Battenberg, felt that he had no alternative but to resign. Within the Royal Navy he was highly respected and regarded as being the best man for the job, but as the ultimate responsibility was his, given that the contemporary code of personal honour differed greatly from that considered to be acceptable today, he was placed in an impossible situation. This was aggravated by his family name having retained its German origins, a fact seized upon by those who hinted that his heart may not have been in the current struggle, a suggestion which was as far from the truth as it was possible to get. Despite this, it was considered advisable that the family should change its surname to Mountbatten.

Prince Louis' successor was Admiral Lord John Fisher, who was brought out of retirement. Fisher is universally regarded as the father of the modern Royal Navy. It was he who introduced the dreadnought battleship and the battle cruiser, and he who was responsible for changing the Navy's basic fuel from coal to oil. Unfortunately, he was also a man who made enemies easily and he was a bad enemy to have, being quite capable of using underhand methods to defeat a perceived opponent. During Queen Victoria's day he conducted a bitter and frequently public feud with Admiral Lord Charles Beresford. At one period an officer named Doveton Sturdee had been appointed Beresford's Chief of Staff. Fisher had asked him to report secretly to him whatever Beresford was doing. Quite properly, Sturdee had declined and Fisher had never forgiven him. Now a Vice Admiral, Sturdee had served as Battenberg's Chief of Staff and he was willing to serve under Fisher in that capacity also. Fisher's intense dislike boiled over immediately. He promptly informed Churchill that he was 'not prepared to tolerate that damned fool as Chief of Staff at the Admiralty for one day longer.'

At length, Churchill managed to calm him down. Sturdee could not be dismissed without some suspicion arising that he was involved in the Coronel debacle. The First Lord pointed out that Sturdee was anything but a fool and that he was particularly noted for his grasp of tactics. The immediate priority was to destroy Spee's squadron before it could break out into the Atlantic. To that effect Stoddart's cruisers were being reinforced with two battle cruisers as this would place Spee at the same disadvantage that Cradock had been faced with at Coronel. Sturdee, Churchill insisted, was the man for the job. Finally, Fisher agreed, accepting that this was the best solution for everyone involved.

Initial reluctance to deprive the Grand Fleet of two such powerful units was muted by the urgency of a situation that demanded Spee's immediate elimination. Sturdee, undoubtedly pleased to exchange the hothouse which the Admiralty had become for the fresher atmosphere of a sea command, hoisted his flag in Captain P.T.H. Beamish's *Invincible* on 9 November. Two days later, accompanied by *Inflexible*, the latter under the command of Captain R.F. Phillimore, she sailed from Devonport and headed south. On 11 November the two battle cruisers reached St Vincent, where they spent twenty-four hours coaling before continuing their journey.

In the meantime, in the immediate aftermath of Coronel, *Glasgow* and *Otranto* had successfully broken contact with the enemy and were

Poorly phrased since Port Stanley is in the Falklands

heading separately for the Horn to reach Port Stanley with the object of reaching the Falkland Islands in the South Atlantic. Aboard the battleship *Canopus,* Captain Grant received a signal from the *Glasgow* to the effect that *Good Hope* and *Monmouth* had been lost with all hands. He decided that in the circumstances his best course of action was to remain in the area until the remnant of Cradock's squadron had reached safety, holding off Spee's ships if they attempted to pursue. As we know, they did not and on 6 November *Canopus* was joined by *Glasgow* in Lomas Bay where word was received that *Otranto* had rounded the Horn safely.

When *Otranto* reached Port Stanley it was decided that she could not contribute much to the defence of the Falklands base and she was despatched to patrol to the north. *Glasgow's* arrival involved some diplomatic sleight of hand that resulted in the light cruiser having her battle damage repaired in a Rio de Janeiro floating dock over a five-day period at Brazilian expense, despite vigorous protests from the German residents. For the moment, therefore, the defence of Port Stanley depended upon Captain Grant's *Canopus.* The old battleship was beached so that her four turret-mounted 12-inch guns could fire over the low southern headland and also cover the harbour mouth. Simultaneously, her secondary armament, consisting of twelve 6-inch guns, was taken ashore and dug into emplacements where they would be manned by the ship's Marines and local volunteers raised by the Governor.

Once her repairs had been completed *Glasgow* joined Rear Admiral Stoddart's cruiser squadron. This now consisted of the armoured cruiser *Carnarvon* (flag, *Defence* having been despatched to South Africa), under the command of Captain H.L. d'E. Skipwith; the armoured cruisers *Kent* (Captain J.D. Allen) and *Cornwall* (Captain W.M. Ellerton), sister ships to the ill-fated *Monmouth*; and the light cruisers *Bristol* (Captain B.H. Fanshaw) and *Glasgow*; plus the armed merchant cruiser *Macedonia*. On 26 November the two British battle cruisers joined the squadron off Abrolhos Rocks and Sturdee assumed command of the combined force with Stoddart as his deputy. Luce requested an interview with Sturdee, recommending that they should proceed as quickly as possible to the Falklands. The admiral accepted his point but was determined to fight the coming battle with sufficient fuel in his bunkers and adequately trained gun crews. Having left Albrohos on 3 December, he proceeded south at just 10 knots, well below his ships' average cruising speed. He also spent a day at gunnery practice, involving an unforeseen delay of twelve hours when divers had to clear the target towing wire which had fouled one of *Invincible's* propellers. It was not until 7 December that the Falklanders were able to heave a sigh of relief as they watched the long line of battle cruisers and cruisers close the coast of East Falkland and enter Port Stanley harbour.

Despite the fact that she had not been sighted for over a month, the *Karlsruhe* was still believed to be active in the general area of the West Indies, while the armed merchant cruiser *Kronprinz Wilhelm* was still at large in the Atlantic. Even together, however, they were only capable of inflicting a fraction of the damage that lay within the power of Spee's East Asia Squadron. The problem was that no one knew quite where Spee was or where he was heading. As a professional he would not have been unduly surprised to learn that thirty Allied warships, British, Australian, French and Japanese, were scouring the world's oceans for him. In fact, his squadron had reached Port Santa Elena and remained there until 6 December, topping up its colliers from a captured British barque, the *Drummuir*.

Prior to sailing on 6 December, Spee held a Captains' conference. He had already made the decision to round the Horn and the question under discussion now was what to do next. The Berlin Admiralty had issued general orders that he should pursue cruiser warfare, that is, preying upon the enemy's commerce, but sinking unarmed merchantmen did not suit his temperament at all. His instinct was to damage or destroy his opponents' ability to fight at all. Intelligence reports suggested that that there was no British naval activity in the area of the Falkland Islands and, naturally being unaware that this situation would change with twenty-four hours, he based his plans on this. He therefore proposed destroying the islands' radio station and coal stocks and, for good measure, kidnapping the Governor in retaliation for the British imprisonment of the captured German Governor of Samoa. The attack would be made by the *Gneisenau* and the *Nurnberg*, with the remainder of the squadron providing distant cover.

The idea received a lukewarm response, being supported only by Spee's Chief of Staff and Schonberg of the *Nurnberg*. It was opposed by the captains of the *Gneisenau, Dresden* and *Leipzig* and, perhaps understandably, Schultz of the *Scharnhorst* does not seem to have expressed an opinion either way. Those objecting to the plan pointed out that the results of the attack did not justify revealing the squadron's presence. They doubted the value of the intelligence regarding the Royal Navy's absence from the Falklands and pointed out that if the islands were bypassed far to the south the squadron would preserve the secrecy surrounding its presence. The squadron could then proceed north up the Atlantic and swing west into the busy shipping lanes of the Plate, where havoc could be caused before it disappeared for a second time. Spee would have none of it and insisted that the attack should proceed. The die had now been cast irrevocably and shortly after the squadron weighed anchor.

To the south of Port Stanley was an area of high ground known as Sapper Hill. On this a lookout post had been constructed, connected to the *Canopus* by land line. At 07.45 on 8 December one of the lookouts spotted a smudge of smoke on the horizon to the south. He called the Officer of the Watch aboard *Canopus,* who in turn alerted Captain Grant. While the details remained unclear, it was known that there were no British ships in the area and the newcomers must, perforce, be hostile. The Enemy in Sight signal soared up the halyards.

Within the harbour, Sturdee's ships were busy about their business. *Carnarvon* and *Glasgow* had finished coaling while *Kent, Cornwall* and *Bristol* still had to wait their turn with the two colliers, although *Kent* could produce a head of steam in less than two hours. The colliers had been moored alongside *Invincible* and *Inflexible* since 04.00, and in the intervening period 400 tons of coal had been transferred to each of the battle cruisers. *Cornwall* and *Bristol* both had parts of their engines stripped down, and the squadron was therefore far from ready for action. At 07.56 the bang of one of *Glasgow's* guns drew everyone's attention to the signal flying from *Canopus's* masthead. At 08.00 Sturdee learned from the lookout post on Sapper Hill that the strangers were a four-funnelled and a two-funnelled warship on a bearing south–eastwards from Port Stanley and steering north.

If there was one characteristic for which Sturdee was famous it was his imperturbability. He ordered *Kent* to proceed outside the harbour entrance and recalled *Macedonia* from beyond it, where she had been acting as guard ship. The colliers would cast off from the battle cruisers and all his ships would raise sufficient steam for 12 knots. Then he went to breakfast. Emerging at 08.45 he was pleased to see that *Kent* was on the move, although it would obviously be some time before the rest of his ships could follow. At 09.00 Sapper Hill reported not only that the two enemy ships were now less than 8 miles distant but also that two more groups of ships had been sighted in the distance. These, of course, were the remainder of Spee's squadron and its three supply ships. There could no longer be any doubt that Spee intended to attack Port Stanley.

Sturdee ordered *Canopus* to open fire as soon as the *Gneisenau* and *Nurnberg* came within range of her guns. At 09.20 the Sapper Hill lookout reported that the enemy had trained his guns on the radio station. At about the same time *Canopus* opened fire at a range of 13,500 yards and, despite being aground, earned her place in history. A long standing rivalry existed between the crews of her fore and aft turrets and when, the previous evening, Grant had ordered a practice shoot the latter decided that they were going to win by fair means or foul. During the night they crept into their turret and loaded the gun's practice shell. Confronted with a real enemy next morning, they had no time to rectify the position. The result was that the fore turret's shells exploded as they hit the water short of the target, but one of the aft turret's practice shells ricocheted and punched a hole in *Gneisenau's* rearmost funnel. Horrified, Captain Maerker swung his ship away to the east and *Nurnberg* conformed. *Canopus* fired again, only to see her entire salvo splashing down even further from the target. Sturdee instructed Grant to cease firing and Maerker resumed his original course on Port Stanley, this time with his battle ensigns flying. Almost immediately he received a signal from Spee, ordering him to avoid action and proceed east by north at full speed. By 09.30 Port Stanley was no longer in any danger.

A situation had existed in which Spee might well have been able to inflict serious damage on some, at least, of Sturdee's ships before they could clear the harbour, so why had he decided to abandon his attack? Two explanations present themselves. This first is that he believed that the two salvos fired by *Canopus* had actually been fired by *two* battleships and he was not prepared to engage against such odds. The second was that he believed his squadron possessed sufficient speed to out-distance any pursuit. His supply ships were ordered to proceed to a given rendezvous and Maerker was instructed to come round on to a south-easterly course. By about 11.00 the German cruisers had formed a line ahead on that heading with *Gneisenau* leading, then *Nurnberg*, then *Scharnhorst*, then *Dresden* and finally *Leipzig*, doing their best to work up to 22 knots.

Back in Port Stanley harbour, *Glasgow* had begun to move at 09.45, followed at 10.00 by Stoddart in *Carnarvon*, followed by *Inflexible*, then Sturdee in *Invincible,* then *Cornwall*. Last to clear at 11.00 was *Bristol*, which had been at longer notice to raise steam. The enemy ships might no longer be visible in themselves, but columns of smoke less than 20 miles distant on the south-eastern horizon clearly indicated their position. As *Inflexible* and *Invincible* were capable of 27 knots it would only be a matter of three or four hours before they overhauled the German squadron. Without hesitation, Sturdee sent the General Chase order soaring up his signal halyards.

As the British began to close the gap, details of their ships became clear to Spee. In a moment of sheer horror he realised that the two largest were each equipped with two tripod masts. That could only mean that they were battle cruisers, mounting heavier guns than anything he could reply with and considerably faster than any of his own ships. He was now in precisely the same position that Cradock had been in at Coronel in that he could neither fight nor flee. When, at 12.47, the British battle cruisers opened fire at the maximum range of 16,500 yards and closing, it was apparent to him that it would only be a matter of time before the trailing *Leipzig* received fatal damage. In the circumstances he took the decision to maintain his south-easterly course with *Scharnhorst* and *Gneisenau* in the hope that the entire British squadron would continue to pursue them, and ordered his light cruisers to break away to the south in the hope that they would escape and continue the war in the Pacific. To Maerker, who had been one of those who had opposed the attack on Port Stanley, he despatched a rueful signal to the effect that he had been proved right after all.

Observing the German light cruisers peeling away to the south, Sturdee read his opponent's mind and, with the exception of *Carnarvon* and *Bristol*, despatched his own cruisers after them while he pursued *Scharnhorst* and *Gneisenau* with *Invincible* and *Inflexible*, followed by the slower *Carnarvon*. Simultaneously, *Macedonia* was ordered out of Port Stanley to join *Bristol* in the pursuit of the German supply ships. There were, therefore, three separate actions taking place at the same time.

The major duel took place between the opposing heavyweights, with *Invincible* engaging *Scharnhorst* and *Inflexible* exchanging broadsides with *Gneisenau*. Initially, Sturdee found himself to be at something of a disadvantage in that he held the lee position. This meant that the dense clouds of smoke belched by his guns, to say nothing of his funnel smoke, was carried by the wind between the opposing ships so that he was uncertain whether his fire was taking effect or not. On the other hand, the Germans were able to observe their own shell splashes and adjust their fire accordingly. Among the British there was universal admiration for the high standard of the enemy's gunnery. Fire control was such that the German guns seemed to fire together with accurate grouping around their targets that the British ships were straddled regularly.

Sturdee's intention was to fight the battle at the range of his own guns and beyond that of his opponent until the latter's fighting capacity had been seriously reduced, but at 13.44 *Invincible* sustained a hit, which fortunately did little damage. Nevertheless, this was not a welcome situation and he swung away to port in order to open the range. Spee surprised him by turning south so that Sturdee had no alternative but to catch up with him once again. Consequently, firing ceased at 14.00 and was not resumed until 14.45. At 14.55, Spee turned towards the British ships until the range had been reduced to 10,000 yards. This not only enabled him to bring his 8.2-inch guns into action, but also his 5.9-inch secondary armament.

At this stage, Sturdee had no idea of the damage that had been inflicted on the enemy, although it was considerable. He now had two important priorities to attend to. First, he must open the range once more, and second, he must fight from a position at which the enemy was clearly visible. At 15.15 he achieved both by swinging away sharply through 32 points until his battle cruisers had crossed the enemy's wake and now had his ships to port at a distance of 14,000 yards, having exchanged targets.

It now became apparent that while the German cruisers were still firing, they had suffered severely. *Scharnhorst* had been hit below the water line both fore and aft and numerous fires were blazing along her length, their smoke mingling with steam pouring from ruptured lines. One by one, her four funnels were shot away or blasted askew like skittles in a bowling alley, starting with the third at 15.30. *Carnarvon,* Stoddart's flagship, had now caught up with the action after being some 10 miles behind at one stage. Her commander, Captain Skipwith, had flogged her engines hard and taken advantage of the various tactical changes of direction taken by the combatants to steer a reasonably straight course and so recover much of the lost mileage. Shortly before 16.00 she was able to add the fire of her four 7.5-inch guns to those already battering the *Scharnhorst.* Despite her damage, the German cruiser had continued to fire steadily but suddenly all her remaining guns fell silent. While her ammunition must have been all but exhausted the more probable explanation for this is that the order to abandon ship had been given. The British ships also ceased firing although the enemy's ensign was still flying. At 16.04 *Scharnhorst* gave a sudden lurch to port as though one of her critical bulkheads had given way, releasing damned up water throughout the hull. A heavy list developed rapidly until she was lying on her beam ends. At 16.17 she slid beneath the waves. Even if those of her crew who managed to swim clear of the ship before she vanished cannot have survived for long in a sea temperature of just 38 degrees. Consequently, there were no survivors as Sturdee's clear duty now lay in dealing with the *Gneisenau,* which was still full of fight.

The German cruiser, in little better state than her lost sister ship, tried to make off to the south-west, but now she was having to absorb the combined fire of three opponents at a range of 10,000 yards. Wreathed in smoke and flames, her foremast leaning at a drunken angle and three of her four funnels holed or blown out of line, she struggled vainly to escape to the south-west with her speed reduced to 16 knots because of damage to her boiler rooms, *Gneisenau* nevertheless continued to fight with the one gun left to her until that, too, fell silent. By 17.50, however, she was lying dead in the water and listing slowly but steadily to starboard. Sturdee ordered his ships to cease firing and lower their boats to pick up survivors. At 18.00 *Gneisenau* went down, the site marked by debris and wisps of steam and smoke that continued to reach the surface. Some of those who managed to leave the ship safely were so weakened by the cold that they were unable to swim for long and drowned before they could be hauled into the boats, but 190 out of the 765-strong crew were rescued. One of the rescued officers, related by marriage to Stoddart, solicitously enquired after the admiral's health.

British casualties during this phase of the battle were negligible. *Invincible* sustained twenty-two hits, mostly with 8.2-inch calibre shells, which had wrecked the wardroom and several ratings' mess decks. One 4-inch gun had been put out of action and a bunker flooded, but there were no personnel casualties. *Inflexible* had one man killed and two slightly wounded but the three hits she had sustained caused little or no damage.

Away to the west, the German light cruisers had become the prey in a high speed chase in which the odds were stacked against them. It was not just that two of their pursuers, *Cornwall* and *Kent*, were armoured cruisers armed with fourteen 6-inch guns apiece as opposed to the German ten 4.1-inch guns each, the boilers and engine rooms of the *Leipzig* and *Nurnberg* were in urgent need of an overhaul after their long stint in the Pacific. Only the *Dresden,* having sustained less wear and tear, stood any chance of out-pacing her British opponents, and then only by a knot or two.

When the British cruisers had turned out of line ahead to an approximate line abreast they acted on Sturdee's order to pursue their opposite numbers, *Kent* was on the left, *Cornwall* was in the centre and *Glasgow* on the right. Captain Ellerton of the *Cornwall* suggested that he should engage *Leipzig* while *Kent* tackled *Nurnberg* and *Glasgow* continued the pursuit of *Dresden*, which was drawing away. Luce, commanding *Glasgow*, was the senior captain present and he did not agree. He not only doubted whether his ship could overhaul *Dresden* before nightfall, but also whether *Cornwall* could catch *Leipzig*. He was himself already exchanging shots with the latter with the intention of slowing her down sufficiently for *Cornwall* to close the gap.

At 14.50 Luce opened fire at 12,000 yards and at 15.10 one of his shells punched its way through *Leipzig's* upper deck and exploded in a bunker that was in use. The result was a temporary reduction in the German ship's speed. Despite this, a running fight was maintained for an hour, by which time the range had closed to 9,000 yards and *Glasgow* had herself been hit twice. Luce was uncertain how much damage he was inflicting on the enemy and, quite correctly, declined to close the range even further. He was, for example, unaware that one of his shells had started a blaze near *Leipzig's* stern which Captain Haun's damage control parties were unable to contain, but he was aware that when *Kent* steamed past her in pursuit of *Nurnberg* she opened fire on her with her hitherto disengaged battery.

By 16.17 *Cornwall* was in range and opened fire. *Leipzig* was now under fire from both British cruisers. She continued to fight back, ignoring *Glasgow* and concentrating her entire effort on *Cornwall*. By 19.30 her foretopmast and mainmast had been shot away, fires were raging throughout the ship and her guns had fallen silent. Haun, having received a report to the effect that all her ammunition had been shot off, ordered three torpedoes to be launched. None found a target as the British ships were outside their range.

Haun decided to scuttle his ship rather than have her fall into enemy hands. The sea cocks were opened and his men assembled on the after part of the forecastle, the only space that was not littered with wreckage or rendered untenable by raging fires. Nevertheless, the ensign still flew and he had no intention of lowering it. He tried to ensure that the wounded were equipped with life jackets, then thanked the crew for their efforts, calling for three cheers for the Kaiser, which were willingly given. Sensing that the end was near, the men broke into a popular patriotic song, *The Song of the Flag*.

In the gathering dusk no one aboard either *Glasgow* or *Cornwall* can have known what was taking place aboard the *Leipzig,* but they did know that while her guns had fallen silent she had not surrendered. They closed in to fire their final broadsides into her. Shells bursting against the armoured gun shields and conning tower sent white-hot splinters ripping through the men crowded on the forecastle, causing heavy loss of life. Some of the men jumped overboard and tried to swim to the British ships but the distance was too great and they were quickly overcome by cold and a rising sea. At 20.30 Luce lowered his boats and signalled the *Leipzig* that he had done so. As she filled with water the German cruiser began listing to port and going down by the bows. Haun gave the order to abandon ship but was still aboard her when she went down. Only seven officers and eleven men were saved from a crew of 285. *Leipzig* had fought alone against impossible odds for four hours, earning the admiration of her foes and regret that the loss of life had been so heavy. In his report, Ellerton expressed his sincere regret that it had not been possible to save as gallant an officer as Haun had proved himself to be. During the action, *Glasgow* sustained the loss of one man killed and two wounded, while *Cornwall* had no personnel casualties and damage limited to two flooded bunkers.

Meanwhile, *Kent* had continued her pursuit of *Nurnberg*. So determined was Captain Allen to catch her that every available piece of wood, including lockers, ladders, capstan bars and even hen coops were broken up and passed down to the stokeholds, where they were flung into the roaring furnaces. Repeatedly, the voice pipe from the bridge demanded more and more speed. Anxious engineer officers watched the needles on their gauges climb until the engines were producing 5,000 more horsepower than the makers claimed they were capable of. Finally, *Kent* was bounding along at 25 knots and steadily overhauling her opponent.

At 17.00 *Nurnberg* opened fire at a range of 12,000 yards. Nine minutes later *Kent* found the range and a running fight ensued in which both ships displayed a high standard of gunnery. With the range down to 7,000 yards *Nurnberg* turned to port in order to bring her entire port battery into action. Allen conformed so that all his starboard guns could reply and set *Kent* on a converging course. As the range closed to 3,000 yards both ships continued to fire steadily but *Nurnberg* was absorbing the greater punishment.

During the engagement a German shell exploded against the gun port of the A3 casemate. The flash set fire to charges inside the casemate and the flames spread down the hoist and would have ignited a charge at the bottom if it had not been flung out of harm's way by Sergeant Charles Mayes, Royal Marine Light Infantry, who then flooded the compartment. If the charge had ignited the flames could have spread along the ammunition passage into the magazine and caused an explosion that would have blown the ship apart. Sergeant Mayes' presence of mind earned him the Conspicuous Gallantry Medal.

At 18.02 both ships turned to starboard. The range opened to 4,000 yards but *Nurnberg's* speed was falling away and she was on fire forward. Ten minutes later Allen invoked a manoeuvre from the days of sail, swinging *Kent* across *Nurnberg's* bows at little over 3,000 yards and raking her with all his starboard guns. He then turned hard a' starboard until he was off the German ship's port bow and battered her with his port guns. By 18.30 *Nurnberg* was barely moving and her guns were silent. Allen ordered his own guns to cease firing but observing that the declined to haul down his colours in surrender and was apparently in no immediate danger of sinking he instructed them to open fire once more.

After five minutes *Nurnberg* struck her colours. She was listing to starboard and starting to settle by the stern. Allen called away his boats but they had been extensively holed by shell splinters and it took the ship's carpenters twenty minutes hard work to get a cutter and a gig into a condition in which they could be launched. Shortly before *Nurnberg* rolled to starboard and slowly sank a group of men were seen on her quarterdeck waving a German ensign nailed to a pole. In total, the boats picked up twelve men, of whom only seven survived their injuries and immersion. Captain von Schonberg was not among them. *Kent's* casualties during the engagement amounted to four men killed and twelve wounded. No serious damaged had been sustained but an enemy shell had passed through the radio office and wrecked the transmitter, so Allen was unable to inform Sturdee of the situation.

Many miles to the south-west, *Dresden* had vanished like a ghost into the drizzle and mist of the South Atlantic evening. Looking astern, her crew watched the gun flashes on the horizon become fewer in number and then finally stop. The radio operators, monitoring the British frequencies, were able to inform Captain Ludecke that *Scharnhorst* had been lost, as had *Gneisenau* and *Leipzig*. Of *Nurnberg* there was no news, nor could she be raised on the radio.

There remained only the three German colliers, *Seydlitz*, *Baden* and *Santa Isabel*. While they attempted to make a run for it, they could not hope to escape from the faster *Bristol* and *Macedonia*. Having surrendered at 15.00, the crews of *Baden* and *Santa Isabel* were transferred to *Macedonia,* to be taken into Port Stanley later. Fanshawe of the *Bristol* then commenced to sink both ships by gunfire, which took until 21.30. During the gathering darkness the faster *Seydlitz* had broken away to the north and found sanctuary in the Argentine port of San Antonio where, in due course, the authorities interned her. While it was true that Sturdee's standing orders required Fanshawe to destroy transports, he was also instructed to take advantage of any opportunity that might arise to capture the enemy's colliers. Thus, inexplicably, he had sent two valuable cargoes to the bottom.

When the final reckoning was made it was clear that Spee had died during the battle, as had his two sons Heinrich and Otto, serving as lieutenants aboard, respectively, *Gneisenau* and *Nurnberg*. The battle had been as complete a victory as any and the Admiralty granted the sum of £12,160 as prize money, to be shared among the battle cruisers and cruisers. The battleship *Canopus,* which had fired the first shots, received not a penny, despite Captain Grant's representations. Sturdee received messages of congratulation from King George V, Admiral Lord Jellicoe on behalf of the Grand Fleet, the French and Russian Admiralties, and his old chief, Admiral Beresford.

The battle cruisers, which had expended most of their main armament ammunition, were summoned home as a matter of urgency and received a hero's welcome. Sturdee was received by the King, created a baronet and was given command of one of the Grand Fleet's battle squadrons. Fisher's response was unbelievably sour and petty. When Sturdee reported to the Admiralty on his return from the Falklands, Fisher kept him waiting for several hours before granting him a five minute interview. Yet, try as he might, was unable to dent Sturdee's popularity.

Nevertheless, while Admiral Spee's East Asia Squadron had ceased to exist, elements of it were still at large and capable of inflicting serious damage.

CHAPTER 6

Ghost Ship

Following the almost complete destruction of Spee's East Asia Squadron, Sturdee's two battle cruisers were ordered to return home immediately. That left Stoddart's cruisers to patrol the South Atlantic and the south-eastern coast of South America, although these would be joined shortly by other warships, including the battle cruiser *Australia*. The survival of the *Dresden*, however, and to a lesser extent that of the armed merchant cruiser *Prinz Eitel Friedrich*, caused Stoddart and the Admiralty serious concern. The root of the problem was that no one seemed to have any idea where *Dresden* might be lurking and British traffic along the Chilean coast was at a virtual standstill. The southern portion of that coastline consisted of such a labyrinth of bays, inlets, fjords, headlands, capes and islands that searching for a single ship was like looking for the proverbial needle in a haystack. Stoddart was looking but having no success at all. At the Admiralty some thought that *Dresden* might be in hiding elsewhere, perhaps even in the East Indies, an alternative that would place the Australian and New Zealand trade routes at risk. At a time when British warships were being withdrawn to home waters, this would not be a welcome addition to available resources. Fisher, never one to lose an opportunity to plunge a knife into an enemy's back, took full advantage of *Dresden's* escape. 'If the *Dresden* gets to the Bay of Bengal by means of colliers arranged with Berlin, we shall all owe a lot to Sturdee,' was his vindictive comment.

In fact, the answer was a lot simpler. She changed her position regularly and was living a sort of hand-to-mouth existence on fuel supplies and rations supplied locally by an efficient organisation known as the *Etappendienst* (roughly, Service Organisation), which had been set up throughout South America on the outbreak of war to keep German ships supplied. In Chile there were some 28,000 immigrants of German origin, most living in small agricultural settlements close to the coast, but others were prominent members of the diplomatic, banking and business circles in cities like Santiago and Valparaiso and were eagerly recruited into the *Etappendienst's* intelligence section. There were also some 4,000 former citizens of the Austro-Hungarian Empire, but as many of them hailed from Dalmatia and had little liking for the Vienna establishment, they were not considered to suitable material for recruitment. Against this, there were a number of neutral ship owners and masters only too happy to pocket German gold in exchange for partisan favours.

The British residents in Chile were at something of a disadvantage in these matters as they were smaller in numbers and more widely dispersed, the only community similar to that of the German settlements being a tiny Welsh community over the border in Argentine Patagonia. However, the *Etappendienst* made little attempt to conceal its own activities and carried out its work in so brazen a manner that British intelligence was able to accumulate so much evidence that by the end of November 1914 it became possible to lodge the strongest possible diplomatic protests. Non-German public opinion in Chile was outraged and the government had no wish to be seen as hostile to the United Kingdom. This placed a brake on the activities of the *Etappendienst* but was unable to halt them altogether.

Aboard the *Dresden*, Captain Ludecke wondered just how much the Berlin Admiralty expected him to achieve. Her presence was clearly affecting the movements of Allied shipping, which was not inclined to leave the safety of neutral harbours. This in itself meant that he was unable to prey on it, which was frustrating in the extreme. Again, while the *Etappendienst* could supply provisions and a limited quantity of coal, replenishing the cruiser's magazine with 4.1-inch shells was beyond its powers. In fact, Ludecke had almost no main armament ammunition left, and certainly not enough for a prolonged engagement.

Following *Dresden's* escape from the Battle of the Falklands, Ludecke had brought her round the Horn into the Pacific at midnight on 8 December. On the afternoon of 9 December he anchored her in Sholl Bay, Tierra del Fuego, to cut sufficient wood to replenish his fuel. Two days later a Chilean destroyer arrived and reminded him that as a combatant he had exceeded the twenty-four hours that belligerent warships were allowed to remain in neutral waters. He therefore up-anchored and proceeded to Punta Arenas, where he arrived on 12 December. The local authorities told him he could stay as long as was necessary to refill his coal bunkers, contravening government orders that *Dresden* was not to be allowed into the port on any account. In the event, Ludecke cut short his stay and put to sea again at midnight on 13 December.

That was the last most people heard of *Dresden* for many weeks. For the next fortnight she hid in Hewitt Bay, then moved to Weihnacht Bay. On 19 January 1915 a supply ship, the *Sierra Cordoba*, joined her there. In Ludecke's opinion, she was not carrying sufficient coal for him to resume the role of a surface raider. In fact, the *Etappendienst* had despatched no less than five colliers that would enable him to strike wherever he wanted. These were the *Gladstone, Josephina, Eleana Woorman, Bangor* and *Gottia*, but for a variety of reasons none of them would reach him. The crew of the *Gladstone* disliked the risks involved in their work and mutinied even before they had rounded the Horn; *Josephina* was captured by the *Cornwall* near the Falkland Islands; *Eleanore Woorman* tried to run for it when challenged by the *Australia* and was sunk by gunfire in the same area; while *Bangor* and *Gottia* sailed, respectively, from Baltimore and Buenos Aires too late to play a part in subsequent events. On 21 January 1915 Ludecke received a signal from Berlin suggesting that he should try returning to Germany by following the same route as sailing vessels. One suspects the Kaiser's involvement in the suggestion, which was hopelessly adrift from reality. The fact was that numerous sailing vessels of different nationalities would be encountered along the way *Dresden* would be identified, reported and tracked down. Ludecke replied that his engines were now in such a poor state that they would be unable to produce anything like the speed required to break through the Royal Navy's North Sea blockade.

On 6 February Ludecke steamed *Dresden* into Quintepeu Fjord in the Gulf of Ancud. As the ship slipped through the narrow entrance to the fjord between towering cliffs that soared 1,500 feet above the level of the water, the rattle and clatter from her over-worked machinery filled the space with harsh echoes. When daylight began to fade a flotilla of sailing craft, assembled by the *Etappendienst* and led by a prominent German-Chilean merchant, Senor Enrique Oelkers, entered the fjord and berthed alongside the cruiser. Entire families had brought with them supplies, coal and some good things that had become just memories to *Dresden's* seamen, including beer, sausages and strudel. Musical instruments were produced and a party followed. Oelkers had brought along several mechanics and they set to immediately, doing what they could to effect necessary repairs in the engine room. Some parts that could not be repaired on the spot were shipped to Puerto Montt and Calbuco, where facilities for their restoration existed.

On 14 February the pleasant interlude came to an end. Repaired and refuelled, *Dresden* and *Sierra Cordoba* pushed out into open water through a howling blizzard, leaving behind a persistent legend that they left a wooden box of Mexican treasure, waterproofed in tar. It has yet to be found and perhaps it is as well to remember that sailors' yarns do not always dovetail exactly with naval history. Having reached a point some 200 miles off the Chilean coast, Ludecke turned north in search of prey. His search went unrewarded until 27 February when, 560 miles south-west of Valparaiso, he captured and scuttled the British barque *Conway Castle*, bound for Australia with 2,400 tons of barley aboard.

The fruitless efforts of Stoddart's cruisers to locate *Dresden* had been watched with such amusement by the *Etappendienst* that its operatives decided to introduce a little wry humour. They spread reports that *Dresden* could be found in Last Hope Inlet, the furthest inland of a tangle of fjords reaching northwards from Smyth's Channel. The inlet was searched twice, the only result being that *Bristol* damaged her rudder on an uncharted shoal and had to be dry-docked briefly.

At the end of February Ludecke sent *Sierra Cordoba* into Valparaiso to replenish her coal supply. At this stage he felt reasonably secure, but the truth was that *Dresden* was nearing the end of her career. *Glasgow's* signals officer, Lieutenant Charles Stuart, intercepted a message from the *Etappendienst* to the *Dresden*. During the war's early days a copy of the German signal code had been captured by the Imperial Russian Navy in the Baltic and passed to the British Admiralty. The Admiralty's Room 40 OB had cracked the code in December and was able to inform Stoddart that the *Etappendienst's* message instructed *Dresden* to meet her collier at a point 300 miles west of Coronel on 5 March. *Kent* was promptly ordered into the area but did not reach it until 7 March. There was nothing to be seen and the following morning a heavy fog restricted visibility. During the afternoon the fog lifted, revealing *Dresden* lying some 12 miles to the west. Captain Allen immediately gave chase, working *Kent* up to a speed of 21 knots. *Dresden,* however, was known to be the fastest ship in her class and had benefited from the recent attention of Senor Oelkers and his mechanics. Despite the fact that *Kent's* funnels were glowing red hot and trailing sparks she began to pull away steadily until by 20.00 she was hull down and all that Allen could see of her was her masts and funnel tops. Within an hour she had disappeared completely.

It was decided to shift the search to the remote Juan Fernandez Islands and in particular the island of Mas a Tierra. Three ships were involved – Luce's *Glasgow*, Allen's *Kent* and an armed transport, the *Orama*. At this point Stuart intercepted another message for *Dresden*. When decoded it instructed her to meet another collier at the group's principal island, Mas a Fuera, also known today as Robinson Crusoe Island because for five years it had been the home of Alexander Selkirk, upon whose adventures Defoe had based his story.

Ludecke anchored *Dresden* in the island's Cumberland Bay on 9 March. There was no sign of a collier and he had less than 100 tons of fuel in his bunkers. He received a signal from Berlin granting permission for him to accept internment. The island's governor was informed that he would await the arrival of a Chilean warship so that the necessary formalities could be concluded and sent four of his officers off to Valparaiso in a local sailing ship so that they could retain their freedom.

When the British ships approached the bay on 14 March *Dresden* was still flying the German ensign and had therefore not been interned by the Chilean authorities. *Glasgow* opened fire at 8,400 yards, scoring hits with her first two salvos. *Kent* joined in and *Dresden*, unable to manoeuvre on account of still being anchored, replied to the best of her ability. This was not great as she had so little ammunition left and after three minutes' firing Ludecke sent up a white flag to join his ensign. As this clearly indicated a wish to parley and discuss surrender terms, Luce also gave the order to cease firing.

A boat pulled away from *Dresden* to come alongside *Glasgow*. A smart lieutenant climbed to the deck, punctiliously saluted the quarter deck and the officer of the watch, and introduced himself as Wilhelm Canaris. He was taken to Luce's cabin where he argued courteously for the best terms possible. For his part, Luce could only demand complete surrender as an alternative to sinking. It hardly mattered that no agreement was reached as Canaris had simply been sent to buy time while Ludecke and his crew opened their sea cocks, underwater torpedo tube doors and condensers to let in the sea. When it became obvious that this would take too long to sink the ship, explosive charges were rigged to blow out the bottom of her forward magazine.

As Canaris left it was observed that the German crew were leaving their ship and heading for the shore. Next, the Chilean governor arrived, outraged that the British had flagrantly disregarded his country's neutrality and engaged in a battle against a vessel that was under the protection of his country's flag, to say nothing of damage caused to Chilean property. The last claim was dubious in the extreme as Luce had ensured that the small settlement in the bay was well out of the line of fire. There could, however, be no doubt that in terms of international law he had acted improperly. A suitable apology accompanied by a bag containing £500 in gold as compensation for the 'damage' seemed to dilute the governor's sense of outrage somewhat. At 10.45 a huge explosion erupted aboard the *Dresden* and she began to sink, slowly at first, then rolled over and disappeared.

During the short action eight of *Dresden's* crew had been killed and sixteen wounded. Luce sent the latter to Valparaiso in *Orama* so that they could receive hospital treatment and did not request their internment. Four days after the sinking the British left following the arrival of a Chilean warship to transport the 300 officers and men of *Dresden's* crew to internment on Quiriquina Island in Talcahuano Bay. The *Etappendienst* engineered the escape of several, the most prominent being Lieutenant Wilhelm Canaris who managed to make his way back to Germany, part of the journey allegedly being made through the United Kingdom. This would not have been too difficult as he was fluent in four languages, including English and Spanish, and was given every possible assistance by German merchants in Chile. Having reached England, it would not have been difficult for him to obtain a passage to Holland, Norway or Sweden, all of which were neutral and maintained communications with Germany. He subsequently served as a U-boat commander in the Mediterranean, ending the war with eighteen kills to his credit. In due course he rose to the rank of Admiral and during the Second World War he served as Chief of the Abwehr, the German Military Intelligence Service. On several occasions his position enabled him to frustrate the designs of Hitler and his Nazis, whom he hated. He was arrested in the wake of the July Bomb Plot against Hitler, imprisoned and humiliated, then hung just weeks before the war ended. During his time in office he kept a model of the *Dresden* on his desk as a reminder of a more honourable era.

As for *Dresden* herself, she remained alone on the bed of Cumberland Bay for many years. With the advent of scuba diving as a hobby she began to receive occasional visitors and was then used by the Chilean Navy for diver training. In recent years a team of Chilean and German divers recovered the ship's bell which, in November 2008, was presented by the Chilean government to the German Armed Forces Museum in Dresden. The ship's story caught the imagination of the novelist C.S. Forester and provided the inspiration for his book *Brown on Resolution*, which also deals with the fate of a German cruiser that has escaped from the Battle of the Falklands.

CHAPTER 7

The Swan of the East

In the summer of 1910 His Imperial Majesty's brand new light cruiser *Emden* joined Admiral Graf von Spee's East Asia Squadron off Apia in Western Samoa. In September she continued her voyage to the squadron's home station of Tsingtao. She belonged to the Dresden Class of light cruisers and although she was not quite as fast as *Dresden* herself she possessed fine lines and the light grey, almost white, paint of her hull, offset by the darker grey of her three funnels, attracted admiring glances and led to her being known among the squadron as The Swan of the East.

The subjects of the recently created German Empire did not always welcome their new rulers and this sometimes led to violent insurrection followed by the harsh repression of those involved. As a result of this *Emden* became one of very few warships belonging to the Imperial German Navy to see active service prior to 1914. In December 1910, under the command of Commander Vollerthun, she was despatched in company with *Nurnberg* to Ponape in the German Caroline Islands to assist in suppressing the outbreak of violence known as the Sokehs Rebellion. This had succeeded sufficiently for the rebels to have constructed their own fortifications. *Emden* subjected these to a sustained bombardment with her main armament and then put a landing party ashore to storm them. Resistance was stiff, costing the lives of one officer and several seamen before the position was taken.

By March 1911 the situation in Ponape had quietened down sufficiently for *Emden* to return to Tsingtao. During the rest of the year she visited Samoa and was sent to Shanghai to protect German interests when the Chinese Revolution broke out in the middle of November and the new Republic of China descended into chaos as local warlords seized power. On 5 January 1912 Vollerthun was relieved by Captain von Restorff, who was himself relieved by Commander Karl von Müller in May 1912.

Hardly had Müller settled in than *Emden* was ordered to the island of Yap in the Marianas Group, where the German settlers believed themselves to be under threat. The ship was made very welcome and her presence seemed to overawe the local troublemakers. Although it was appreciated that the interior of the island was still dangerous, the coastal settlement of Citape seemed secure enough and *Emden* returned to Tsingtao. Later that year she was sent to the Yangtze River where warlords were using their troops to impose their will on the river traffic, making a name for herself by silencing a rebel artillery battery that had opened an inaccurate fire on her.

Müller was a quiet, thoughtful man who was able to see the storm clouds of war gathering during the summer of 1914. That July the rest of the squadron was showing the flag in Germany's Pacific colonies and Müller reached the conclusion that Tsingtao would quickly become a trap once war was declared. He therefore took *Emden* to sea on 31 July and learned that his country was at war two days later.

As described elsewhere, the Russian liner *Ryazan* was captured and escorted into Tsingtao where she underwent conversion to an armed merchant cruiser. *Emden* left almost immediately and on 8 August rejoined the East Asia Squadron at the island of Pagan in the northern Marianas. There, Müller convinced Spee that by acting independently in the Indian Ocean he could do the enemy far more damage than would be possible if he remained with the squadron, and simultaneously reduce its logistic burden. On 14 August, accompanied by the fully laden collier *Markomannia*, he left the squadron and commenced one of the most remarkable raiding careers in the history of sea warfare.

Before entering the Indian Ocean, Müller decided to coal in a secluded bay on the coast of Timor in the Dutch East Indies. The work had not been long in progress when it was suspended by the arrival of a more powerful Dutch warship, the 5,300-ton *Tromp*. The Dutch captain courteously explained that the *Emden* was in neutral territorial waters and must leave, although he permitted the coaling to continue until the task was completed. On 28 August Müller took *Emden* through the Lombok Strait between the islands of Bali and Lombok and on into the Indian Ocean with *Markomannia* following several miles behind. At one point *Emden's* radio operators picked up Dutch transmission reporting a violation of territorial water by a four-funnelled British warship. *Emden* had only three funnels and Müller decided to add a dummy fourth, made from wood and canvas, so that she resembled the British cruiser *Yarmouth*. The dummy funnel could be raised and lowered as the situation required.

Within the Indian Ocean convoys were the exception rather than the rule and the vast majority of Allied merchant ships sailed as individuals and without escort. The result was that throughout September *Emden* captured no less than seventeen ships. In this Müller was greatly assisted by one of his reserve officers, Lieutenant Lauterbach, who in peacetime was a merchant skipper familiar with the Far East, its trade routes and shipping patterns. Invariably a round fired across the bows of the intercepted vessel, plus a warning not to use her radio, was sufficient to bring her to a standstill. A boarding party would then strip her of anything that might be useful to the *Emden* and she would then be sunk by gunfire or demolition charges. In this way *Emden* and her colliers managed to live off her victims, absorbing their coal, provisions and luxury items. The crews of captured ships would normally be housed under guard in one of the prizes and when their numbers grew too great they would be despatched into a neutral port and released, where they invariably commented on the chivalrous nature of the raider's commander.

On 10 September *Emden* made her first capture, a Greek collier named *Pontoporus*. The ship was operating under a British charter but her master did not care who he worked for, provided he was paid. Unfortunately, his ship was carrying poor quality Indian coal that was difficult to handle and smoked horribly, which was the last thing Müller wanted. That day also saw the capture of a small freighter, the

Indus, with general cargo aboard. The next day it was the turn of the *Lovat,* sailing in ballast. The *Kabinga*, taken the following day, presented Müller with something of a problem as, while the ship herself was British, the cargo was American property and would have to be paid for if destroyed. In the end, he decided to let her go. Also released was a neutral Italian freighter, the *Dandolo*.

Two captures were made on 13 September. First was the collier *Killin*, loaded with Indian coal. Müller had more than enough of this commodity and sent her to the bottom with gunfire. Next came the *Diplomat*, bound from Calcutta to London with 1,000 tons of tea aboard. This was of no earthly use to the *Emden* and she was quickly disposed of with a combination of demolition charges and opened sea cocks. Two more British ships were captured the following day – the *Trabboch*, in ballast and heading for Calcutta, which was quickly disposed of, and the freighter *Clan Matheson*. The captain of the latter, however, was a belligerent Scot who refused to stop in response to the usual shot across the bows and only did so when warned that the next would be part of a salvo directed at the ship herself. Aboard her were railway locomotives, Rolls-Royce cars and assorted machinery also bound for Calcutta, together with several thoroughbred race horses which had to be shot because it was impossible to accommodate them.

Next along was another Italian ship, the *Lorendano*. In a deal negotiated by one of Müller's officers, Lieutenant Prince Franz Josef von Hohenzollern, her captain undertook to relieve *Emden* of her civilian passengers and convey them to Calcutta, promising faithfully not to reveal the raider's position. On the night of 14 September, however, a clear transmission from the Calcutta lightship gave all shipping in the area *Emden's* precise position as recorded by the *Lorendano*, together with details of the ships already sunk by the raider. It seemed, therefore, that the Italian captain's word of honour was completely worthless. The immediate consequence was that marine insurers raised their war rates for the Bay of Bengal and Indian Ocean to prohibitive levels, while masters and ship owners preferred to pay harbour dues rather than risk putting to sea. The Allied authorities, furious that a single cruiser was capable of causing such chaos, demanded action from their respective navies. The result was that British, Australian, French, Japanese and Russian warships began converging on the area.

For the next few days the *Emden's* lookouts scoured the horizon in vain. On 18 September, however, she stopped the neutral Norwegian steamer *Dovre* and transferred the remaining civilian prisoners to her, paying her master 100 Mexican dollars to take them to a safe port, this being the currency in common use at Tsingtao. During their conversation the Norwegian captain mentioned that he had recently left Penang in Malaya, remarking on the presence of two French cruisers, *Montcalm* and *Dupleix*, in the harbour. Müller immediately reached a decision; if the enemy would not come to him, he would go to the enemy. For the moment, Penang could wait as his mind was set on bombarding Madras on the south-east coast of India, which was much closer.

The lack of recent sinkings had generated an entirely false sense of optimism among the Allies, some of whose newspapers reported that the *Emden* herself had been sunk, although no verifiable details were available. Nevertheless, this wishful thinking generated a festive atmosphere in Madras. On the evening of 22 September the lights blazed along the waterfront as they had in peacetime and the only place to be was at a large dinner held at the Madras Club to celebrate the destruction of the raider. Because of this, most of the coast defence artillery batteries were unmanned. At 19.45 Müller brought *Emden* to a standstill some 2,500 yards off the shoreline and ordered her searchlights to be snapped on. They illuminated the Burma Oil Company's storage tanks, at which the guns promptly opened fire. They quickly erupted into smoke and flame and more fires were started in the city beyond by shells that had passed over their target. Ashore, startled coast defence gunners ran to man their weapons but their hasty response was wild and not a shell burst within 100 yards of the cruiser. Then, having fired 125 rounds, *Emden* was gone, disappearing towards the northern horizon. In the Madras Club, there was an outraged rush to the doors when servants politely informed the diners that their city and harbour were ablaze. The fires burned all night and their glow remained visible to *Emden's* crew, now 90 miles out to sea. Naturally, her destructive foray into what were regarded as being British waters created uproar at the highest government levels in London and Delhi. It was not just a question of the damage done, for British prestige had taken so serious a mauling that the frightened Indian population continued to leave Madras for several days after the bombardment. Allied naval commanders were instructed to make every effort to locate and destroy *Emden* but, once again, she had vanished.

Müller had turned south, intending to sink ships in the harbour of the French colony of Pondicherry, only to find it empty. He then decided to prey on the sea lanes off Colombo in the island of Ceylon (Sri Lanka). During the afternoon of 25 September the steamer *King Lud*, sailing in ballast from Suez to Calcutta, was overtaken and sunk. During the evening *Emden* was lying some miles to the west of Colombo, which had apparently taken the lessons of Madras to heart as the coast defence batteries' searchlights were sweeping the surface of the sea outside the naval base. In the event, they proved to be a two-edged sword as at 20.00 a ship was seen to leave the harbour, silhouetted by the roving beams.

Müller put the cruiser on a parallel course and when the two ships were out of the sight of land he ordered the newcomer to heave to. Lieutenant Lauterbach, commanding the boarding party, signalled that she was the *Tymaric*, British, laden with sugar and bound for England. Her skipper, a Captain Tulloch, was incoherent with rage, having been informed by the port captain at Colombo that the *Emden* was nowhere in the area and no danger existed between Colombo and Aden. Müller had intended to sail the ship some distance along her intended course before sinking her, but Tulloch and his chief engineer belligerently refused to sail her and when brought aboard the *Emden* showed a pointed disregard for naval etiquette. Lauterbach caught some of their muttered conversation, which suggested that they intended some sort of coup. Müller was not prepared to take a risk and decided to sink the *Tymaric* with scuttling charges. Her crew were taken off at once, furious at having to leave their belongings behind because of Tulloch's attitude. They came close to lynching him and his chief engineer and were only prevented from doing so by the intervention of their German guards.

Another British freighter, the *Gryfvale*, was taken the following day. After she had been stripped of everything useful the majority of the captured crews were transferred to her and she was released and directed to Cochin. Twenty-seventh of September was one of the busiest in the *Emden's* history. Four ships were intercepted, one of which, the Dutch *Djocja*, was released. Two British ships sailing in ballast, the *Riberra* and the *Foyle*, were sunk, but the collier *Buresk*, loaded with good quality Welsh coal, remained with *Emden* for most of her remaining career. The *Markomannia* and *Pontoporros* were sent off with mail for home and were ordered to procure further supplies of coal, if possible, and rendezvous with *Emden* at a later date. Unknown to Müller they were intercepted by the cruiser *Yarmouth* on 15 October, the former being sunk and the latter sent in to Singapore with a prize crew aboard.

Meanwhile, Müller had decided that *Emden* needed careening to restore her speed and that her hard-worked crew needed rest. He headed south to the lonely Chagos Archipelago which he reached on 5 October. At Diego Garcia, the island group's principal village, the inhabitants were completely unaware that a global war was in progress. For the next ten days essential repairs were carried out to the ship's machinery and the ship was healed first one way and then the other for the barnacles to be scraped off her bottom. During the evening the ship's band got out its instruments and held impromptu concerts.

On 15 October *Emden* headed north to continue her tour of destruction to the west of Cape Comorin, the southernmost point of India. On the same day the steamer *Clan Grant* was stopped, plundered of her tobacco and liquor stores, then sunk. During 16 October a small dredger, the *Pornrabbel*, was intercepted and sunk, the impression being given by her crew being that they were far from sorry to leave their ugly, sluggish, clattering home. Shortly before midnight *Emden* encountered the *Ben Mohr*, laden with machinery and, having taken off the crew, despatched her at once.

The next day passed without incident but on 18 October *Emden* took her greatest prize yet, the 7,500-ton Blue Funnel liner *Troilus*, homeward bound with a full cargo of rubber and metals that would be of immense value to the British war industry. Her captain was extremely angry, having also been informed that the route from Colombo was open, although those using it were advised to proceed thirty miles north of the usual shipping lane. That was exactly what *Troilus* had been doing when *Emden* appeared out of the blue. Her capture actually placed Müller in something of a difficulty. *Buresk* was already crowded with prisoners and for obvious reasons he could not transfer them to *Troilus* and release her as she would waste no time in reporting his position. He needed to capture another cargo/passenger liner quickly and transfer all the prisoners to that before sending *Troilus* and her priceless cargo to the bottom. Some hours later it seemed as though Müller's wish had been granted when a smaller steamer was stopped. Unfortunately, she proved to be a neutral, the Spanish *Fernando Po* and, disinclined to repeat his earlier experience with the talkative Italian captain, Müller sent her on her way. Nevertheless, his luck held and shortly after a British freighter, the *St Egbert*, was run down and captured. Even better was the discovery that she was carrying a neutral cargo bound for New York. He decided that the prisoners would be transferred aboard her but before arrangements could be made for this two more prizes were taken the following day. The first was the collier *Exford*, which Müller decided would accompany the *Emden*, and the second was the British India Steam Navigation Company's steamer *Chilkana*, a brand new ship carrying luxury goods and a fine selection of rations. All the ships' boats now began transferring prisoner and supplies to the *St Egbert* and provisioning the *Emden*, *Buresk* and *Exford*. The *Chilkana* and the *Troilus* were then sunk, the former by means of demolition charges and the latter by gunfire, which took far longer than had been expected. The *St Egbert* was then released with 600 civilian prisoners aboard and instructed to make for an Indian port.

Whenever possible, newspapers were brought aboard the *Emden* from captured ships. They gave the crew some idea of how the war was going elsewhere, but even more interesting were highly coloured accounts of their own doings. To their surprise they found references to themselves in the British press that were far from hostile. It was not just because Müller had chosen to fight a chivalrous war, treating his captives with consideration and releasing them whenever possible; rather it was something in the British psyche that they did not quite understand, namely admiration for a buccaneering spirit that went far back to the days of Drake, Hawkins and a score more. The tone of reporting had changed somewhat recently, the reason being that too many merchant vessels and their cargos were being lost and the insurance war rates for the rest were, for the time being, too high for comfort. What seemed to annoy the British public most was that the combined Allied navies seemed incapable of doing something about the *Emden*. The Admiralty came in for sharp criticism from *The Times* newspaper, an event almost unheard of, and in response issued a plaintive statement to the effect that at this stage of the war there were possibly as many as eight German surface raiders loose in the world's major oceans and that they were being hunted by no less than seventy Allied warships. In response to a request for greater Allied cooperation in the Indian Ocean, more French, Russian and Japanese warships were assisting in the search for the elusive *Emden*. In fact, while those aboard the cruiser were justifiably proud of their achievements they were fully aware that, sooner or later, a more powerful Allied warship would catch up with them and the result would be that many of their lives would be lost.

In the meantime, Müller was aware of the danger of outstaying his welcome in his present area of operations. The earlier mention of Allied warships in Penang had remained with him and he decided to attack the harbour and do as much damage as possible before disappearing again. Penang lay several days' sailing to the east, but this would give the crew a chance to catch up on their rest and put the ship into fighting trim. The voyage passed without incident but on 27 October Müller briefed his officers and men and final preparations for the attack were made, including hoisting the dummy funnel. By 02.00 next morning the lights of Penang were in view. It was Müller's intention to enter the harbour at first light and until then *Emden* cruised slowly up and down. At 04.50 the crew were sent to their action stations. Slowly *Emden* slid into the harbour, her lookouts' eyes probing the grey half light in search of the enemy. Müller had expected the French cruisers *Montcalm* and *Dupleix* to appear be present but there was no sign of them, although a number of destroyers seemed to be present. There was also a larger warship with three squat funnels, which Lauterbach recognised as the Russian light cruiser *Zhemchug*. During his merchant career he had visited her home station, Vladivostok, and been a guest of her captain. He was able to inform Müller that she had the potential to be a dangerous opponent, being armed with eight 4.7-inch guns and three 18-inch torpedo tubes, plus a smaller secondary armament. During the Russo-Japanese War of 1905 she had been present at the Battle of Tsushima where the Russian fleet had been all but destroyed by the Japanese, although she had managed to escape to internment at Manila in the Philippine Islands and subsequently been returned to the Imperial Russian Navy. It was unfortunate that many Russian senior officers of the period took a less than exacting view of their duties. Her present captain, a Baron Cherkassov, conformed to this image and had a mistress in Penang with whom he spent his nights ashore. *Zhemchug*, therefore, was far from being prepared for any sort of action and was running a comfortable peacetime routine. As the light strengthened the ship's steam pinnace left her side and chugged towards the town, taking the cooks to make their purchases as the early morning market. They were the luckiest men in her crew.

Slowly the distance between *Emden* and *Zhemchug* closed to 300 yards, the former now with her battle ensigns flying. At 05.18 *Emden* launched a torpedo from her port-side tube. Suddenly there was a stirring on *Zhemchug's* deck and bridge. Figures were shouting and pointing at the white track of bubbles streaking towards their ship. Within seconds there was an underwater explosion and a huge upsurge of water beside her second funnel. The cruiser seemed to heave herself upwards then settle back, down by the stern.

The Russian officers could be heard yelling at their men to man the guns. The few rounds fired failed to find a target and then *Zhemchug* was blasted and set ablaze by the combined fire of *Emden's* port broadside. Müller was now swinging his ship round to port so that his starboard torpedo tube could bear. Seven seconds after it was launched, her second torpedo exploded against the enemy's hull below the bridge, causing a further explosion in the neighbouring torpedo storage compartment. Once again the cruiser seemed to lift herself clear of the water. Then, broken into two sections she sank immediately, leaving smoking wreckage, jutting masts and the heads of swimming survivors to mark her positions. Of her 350-strong crew, eighty-nine had been killed and 143 wounded during the brief engagement.

In terms of the Allied effort in the Pacific theatre of war, the loss of *Zhemchug* was not a disaster. Only a tiny fraction of Russia's immense population lived near the sea, which was a source of fear to those conscripts who did not. Nor was the relationship between them and their officers a good one, added to which discipline aboard *Zhemchug* was bad. Jacques Mordal relates in his book *25 Centuries of Sea Warfare* that on one occasion she had been accused of firing on the Japanese cruiser *Chikuma*, presumably for old times' sake. Again, gunfire had been heard in Penang harbour during the early hours of the morning of *Emden's* attack and this had been traced to the drunken antics of *Zhemchug's* shore-leave party whose high spirits had led them to bang off a few rounds for fun. In overall terms, the man responsible for this state of affairs was Baron Cherkassov, who was court-martialled for negligence and spent the next three-and-a-half years in prison.

Hardly had *Zhemchug* gone down than machine gun bullets began passing over *Emden* like a swarm of enraged bees. Their source was recognised as being the French destroyer *d'Iberville*, which had served alongside *Emden* at Shanghai. She was partially shielded by a merchant ship and Müller would have been tempted to deal with her had not his attention been distracted by a vessel entering the harbour. He took it to be a torpedo boat and headed towards her at speed, opening fire at 6,000 yards. By the time he recognised that she was simply a pilot boat a hole had been punched through her funnel. He ceased firing at once and headed out to sea.

Aboard *Emden* there was general satisfaction at the outcome of the raid, although the day's fighting was far from over. At 07.00 smoke was sighted to port and the crew returned to action stations. The newcomer turned out to be a merchant ship, the *Glanturret*, flying flags indicating that her cargo was explosives. Müller was on the point of having her sunk by scuttling but was forced to let her go when a small warship unexpectedly began closing in from astern at high speed. Once again, *Emden's* crew went to action stations.

The stranger was the French destroyer *Mousquet* commanded by Lieutenant Theroine. She was returning from a patrol in the Malacca Straits and while she was unaware of what had happened inside Penang harbour, she had had a distant sighting of *Emden* approaching it, the latter's fourth 'funnel' having convinced Theroine that she was British. The same was true when the cruiser left the harbour. Only when he entered the harbour himself did Theroine realised the enormity of his mistake. While the remaining two French destroyers were raising steam he set off in a wild pursuit of *Emden*, convinced that he was on the brink of professional ruin.

It was a hopeless situation. *Mousquet* stood no chance at all against the *Emden*. The latter hoisted her battle ensign anew and opened rapid and destructive fire against her smaller opponent. *Mousquet* bravely replied as best she could, but *Emden's* third salvo knocked out her forward gun, smashed the wireless room in which the operator was broadcasting the news of the cruiser's presence and wrecked the after boiler room. The fourth salvo destroyed the forward boiler room. The little ship's way fell off and, a mere quarter of an hour after the engagement had begun, *Mousquet* put her bows under and sank, still firing. Both of Theroine's legs had been shot off but he had insisted on being strapped into his bridge chair and went down with her. Müller hoisted out his two cutters, which picked up thirty-six survivors, five of whom were so badly wounded that they died shortly after and were accorded the honours of a full naval funeral.

Early on 30 October *Emden* captured the British freighter *Newburn*, bound for Singapore with a cargo of salt. Müller quickly reached an agreement with the *Newburn's* captain and the Frenchmen. The *Newburn* would take the prisoners to Khota Raja, a port in neutral Dutch Sumatra that was believed to contain a modern hospital in which the wounded would receive better treatment, and French gave their parole not to fight against Germany against during the present war.

On 31 October *Emden* met the *Buresk* at the agreed rendezvous and the two ships sailed along the deserted western coast of Sumatra. Some 500 tons of coal were transferred from the collier. *Emden* then penetrated the Sunda Strait, between Sumatra and Java, in search of prey, but found them deserted and headed south west to the Cocos Island. There, on Direction Island, was a most important objective consisting of a British wireless station and a cable relay station at which the cable from Australia to India crossed that from Australia to Zanzibar. The loss of these facilities would obviously cause problems for the British across a huge area.

On the morning of 9 November *Emden* anchored off shore while her First Officer, Lieutenant Commander Helmut von Mücke, led a fifty-strong party ashore and began the work of destruction. *Emden's* dummy funnel was now so tattered that it no longer provided a disguise. The cruiser was recognised by the signal station's staff who began transmitting at once. 'SOS strange ship in entrance' was sent several times together with the station's call sign before it was jammed. It was then changed to 'SOS *Emden* here' and repeated constantly despite the jamming until Mücke burst into the transmitter room and ordered the operators away from their sets at gun point.

What neither Müller nor Mücke knew was that some of the early transmissions had got through before they could be jammed and had been picked up by receivers just 55 miles north of the island, where an escorted convoy of Australian troopships was passing. The convoy's escort consisted of two Australian cruisers, *Melbourne* and *Sydney*, and the Japanese battle cruiser *Ibuki*. The instinct of the escort commander,

Captain Silver, was to engage the *Emden* with his own *Melbourne*, but as she was more powerful than the *Sydney* and the defence of the convoy was his first priority, he decided that the destruction of the enemy must be the responsibility of Captain John Glossop's *Sydney*, which was herself more heavily armed than the *Emden*, possessing eight 6-inch guns with which to oppose the German's ten 4.1-inch.

Ashore, Mücke's landing party was taking longer than expected to complete its work because it was initially unable to locate the point where the cables entered the sea. At 09.15 Müller ordered the ship's sirens to blow the recall signal. As they did so he saw that a ship approaching the island was not the collier *Buresk*, which he had been expecting, but a warship flying the White Ensign. He promptly gave orders for the anchor to be weighed, rang down for full steam to be raised and sent the crew to their action stations. In the circumstances he had no alternative but to abandon Mücke and the landing party. With the anchor secured he immediately steered for the *Sydney*, opening fire at 5,600 yards range. Three salvos straddled the Australian cruiser and the fourth struck, wrecking her fire control system.

Emden had been a lucky ship and with that salvo went the last of her luck. Glossop hauled off to a point at which his guns were within range but *Emden*'s were not. It took his gunners, aiming manually, ten minutes to find the range, and then they began to batter *Emden* to wreckage. Müller strove desperately to get within range but *Sydney* was faster, had thicker armour and managed to stay out of trouble without difficulty. In rapid succession *Emden* sustained hits to her bridge, radio room and mainmast crow's nest and one of the after guns. By 11.00 all the cruiser's funnels were down, the gun control turret had been knocked out and fires were raging, the foremast had toppled, the remaining guns had been silenced, the torpedo flat had been holed and was flooding, the ship was being steered from the steering flat, and the decks were littered with dead, dying and wounded. Müller himself had sustained a slight wound while visiting the main deck, having luckily left the bridge only moments before it was hit. As the ship was no longer capable of fighting he decided to run her aground on the reef of North Keeling Island and so save as many of his men as possible. By 11.15 *Emden* had been run aground with a scream of tortured metal. It was a sad end for the cruiser whose fine appearance had led to her being named The Swan of the East.

Glossop had sighted the approaching *Buresk* and with *Emden* now reduced to a hulk he set off in pursuit of her. The slow collier stood no chance at all and was scuttled by her captain. *Sydney* then returned to *Emden* only to find that she was still flying the German ensign. *Emden's* signal books had been destroyed and when asked whether she had surrendered she could make not make an intelligible reply with her signal lamp. *Sydney* opened fire again but stopped when Müller lowered the ensign and sent up a white flag.

By degrees the wounded were transferred and it became possible to count the cost of the action. *Emden's* losses amounted to 141 killed and sixty-five wounded; only 117 remained unhurt. In contrast, *Sydney* had sustained the loss of only four men killed and seventeen wounded, the majority incurred during the opening minutes of the engagement.

Emden's survivors spent the remainder of the war in a prison camp in Singapore, where they encountered a number of old comrades who had been captured aboard the colliers. In February 1919 Indian and Malay troops forming the local garrison mutinied and invited the Germans to join them. The invitation was refused and the mutiny was put down a week later. Müller and some of his officers had meanwhile been transferred to Malta. Subsequently Müller was moved to London where he remained until October 1918 when he was repatriated under a prisoner exchange scheme. Already a recipient of the Iron Cross, he was presented with Imperial Germany's highest award, the *Pour le Mérite*. He retired from the Navy because of ill health and died unexpectedly in 1923. All of the cruiser's officers received the Iron Cross First Class and fifty of her crew received the Iron Cross Second Class. The Iron Cross was conferred on the ship herself and has been carried on the bows of every subsequent *Emden*.

Meanwhile, after many adventures, Mücke and his landing party had managed to return to Germany. Mücke was generally regarded as a strict disciplinarian, but that was only to be expected of any warship's First Lieutenant. He was also a very capable officer who thought through every difficulty he encountered and managed to produce a solution. He had witnessed the one-sided duel between the *Sydney* and the *Emden* and was well aware that he and his men were now on their own. He had commandeered the *Ayesha*, a schooner belonging to the cable company, and had disappeared by the time *Sydney* turned her attention to Direction Island. He sailed her to Padang in Sumatra where he persuaded the captain of a German merchant ship, the *Choising*, to convey the party to Hodeida in Yemen, which was then a province of the Turkish Empire, believing that a railway from there connected with the famous Hejaz Railway at Medina. Unfortunately, such a railway, though marked on a map, had never been built and although the party reached Hodeida it was forced to sail northwards by zambuk and then travel many miles overland by camel caravan before the main line was reached, being besieged by hundreds of Bedouin tribesmen for several days until relieved by local Turkish troops. The rail journey took them first to Damascus and then on to Constantinople where they received the warmest of welcomes from Admiral Souchon and the crews of the *Goeben* and *Breslau*. From there another train carried them across Europe to Berlin and a tumultuous welcome as heroes. As for *Emden*, little is left as a reminder that she enjoyed one of the most remarkable careers in naval history. The larger part of her wreck was salvaged for scrap in 1950, but one of her guns can still be seen in Hyde Park, Sydney, another at the Australian War Memorial in Canberra, and one her shells is on display in the city museum of Madras.

Prize Log

Ships Captured By *Emden*, Other Than Neutral

Ryasan, 4 August 1914, converted to auxiliary cruiser role at Tsingtao

Pontoporus, 10 September 1914, 4,049 tons, Greek collier, voluntarily entered German service, sunk by HMS *Yarmouth*

Indus, 10 September 1914, 3,393 tons, general cargo, sunk

Lovat, 11 September 1914, 6,102 tons, ballast, sunk

Kabinga, 12 September 1914, 4,657 tons, released 14 September

Killin, 13 September 1914, 3,512 tons, collier, sunk

Diplomat, 13 September 1914, 4,657 tons, general cargo, sunk

Trabboch, 14 September 1914, 4,014 tons, ballast, sunk

Clan Matheson, 14 September, 4,775 tons, general cargo, sunk

King Lud, 25 September 1914, 3,650 tons, ballast, sunk

Tymeric, 25 September 1914, 3,314 tons, sugar, sunk

Gryfevale, 26 September 1914, 4,437 tons, general cargo, released

Buresk, 27 September 1914, 4,350 tons, collier, scuttled to
    prevent re-capture by HMAS *Sydney*

Ribera, 27 September 1914, 4,147 tons, ballast, sunk

Foyle, 27 September 1914, 4,147 tons, ballast, sunk

Clan Grant, 15 October 1914, 3,948 tons, general cargo, sunk

Ben Mohr, 16 October 1914, 4,806 tons, general cargo, sunk

Pornrabbel, 16 October 1914, 473 tons, dredger, sunk

Troilus, 18 October 1914, 7,526 tons, general cargo, sunk

St Egbert, 18 October 1914, 5,526 tons, general cargo, sunk

Exford, 19 October 1914, 4,542 tons, collier, recaptured by HM
    Armed Merchant Cruiser *Empress of Asia*

Chilkana, 19 October 1914, 5,146 tons, general cargo, sunk

Glenturret, 28 October 1914, tonnage not stated, general cargo,
    released

Zhemchug, 28 October 1914, Russian light cruiser, sunk by
    torpedoes and gunfire

Mousquet, 28 October 1914, French destroyer, sunk by gunfire

Newburn, 30 October 1914, released with prisoners from
    Mousquet

Ayesha, 9 November 1914, schooner, used for landing party's
    escape from Direction Island to Padang, Sumatra, then
    scuttled

CHAPTER 8

African Interlude

G ermany was a late starter in what became known as the Scramble for Africa and, despite the Kaiser's claim for what he considered to be his country's rightful 'place in the sun', only managed to acquire a handful of territories in which other powers, notably the United Kingdom, had little or no interest. These included Togoland, Cameroon, South West Africa and German East Africa (Tanga), the last being subsequently known as Tanganyika and then Tanzania.

The Germans were harsh colonial masters, demanding serf-like obedience from their native subjects and inflicting horrific punishments on those who chose to offer resistance. In South West Africa the Herero and Namaqua tribesmen were driven to open rebellion. Having defeated them in the field the German commander, Lieutenant General Lothar von Trotha, promised them extermination and drove them into the Omaheke desert where most of them died of thirst or from the deliberate poisoning of the few wells. It is estimated that some 65,000 Herero and 10,000 Namaqua were killed in this, the first genocide of the twentieth century.

A similar uprising, known as the Maji Maji War, took place in Tanga between 1905 and 1907, despite the colony being more highly developed than South West Africa. Reinforcements were requested and promptly despatched from Germany and the German colony of New Guinea but failed to bring the situation under control. The Governor, Count Gustav von Gotzen, distantly related to a wildly optimistic pretender to the Mexican throne, last sat on briefly by the

Austrian Archduke Maximilian in the 1860s, offered a pardon to those insurgents who abandoned their leaders and witch doctors and handed in their weapons. According to Gotzen's own figures between 200,000 and 300,000 rebels and their supporters died in the rising, while only fifteen German and 389 African soldiers lost their lives.

When war broke out in 1914 Togoland was quickly overrun while the German forces in South West Africa surrendered to South African troops in July 1915. The naval presence of the latter territory had amounted to one small gunboat, the *Eber*, which had been a frequent visitor to Cape Town in time of peace, no doubt to relieve the utter boredom of her home station. War saw the *Eber* vanish into the Atlantic where her guns were transferred to the ocean liner *Cap Trafalgar*, which became a commerce raider while *Eber* sailed on to neutral Brazil and internment. Cameroon held out until February 1916.

However, the German forces in East Africa, including the native *Schutztruppe*, did not surrender until two weeks after the armistice that initiated the process of Germany's surrender. Given what had gone before this might seem surprising, yet since the rebellion Tanga had become the best administered of Germany's colonies. A new Governor, Dr Heinrich Schnee, had instituted a series of social and economic reforms that actually benefited the African population, who now felt that they had something worth fighting for. This enabled the German military commander in the colony, Colonel Paul Emil von Lettow Vorbeck, to build up a formidable force of *Schutztruppe* battalions. Lettow Vorbeck had followed the conventional German path to a commission, having graduated from the famous cadet academies of Kassel and Lichterfeld. He saw active service in China during the Boxer Rebellion and in South West Africa against the Hereros. Thereafter his career took a more individual road. While the ambition of most German officers was to pass through the various stages of regimental life with a view to ultimately securing a staff appointment, he preferred to serve abroad even if this removed him from the mainstream of German military life. At one stage he had commanded a Marine battalion in Wilhelmhaven.

In 1913 Dr Schnee had requested Berlin to replace his modest naval presence – an old gunboat whose engine was still assisted by sails – with something a little more prestigious. The Admiralty agreed and the light cruiser *Konigsberg*, under Commander Max Looff, was despatched from Kiel. Her route took her through the Mediterranean, along the Suez Canal and down the Red Sea to Aden, where, the world still being at peace, Looff paid a courtesy call on the British governor who entertained him to dinner. The cruiser reached Dar es Salaam, the capital of the German colony, on 6 June 1914. She was much admired for her smart turnout and particularly for her three funnels, which were taken by the local population as symbolic of her fighting capacity.

On 29 June the assassination of Austrian Archduke Franz Ferdinand initiated the international slide down the slippery slope to total war. Looff carried out gunnery and torpedo exercises, saw to it that his ship was fully provisioned, landed his wooden furniture and fittings, and detailed the steamer *Somali* as his supply ship in the event of war being declared. It quickly became apparent that the British, fully aware of his presence, were intent on eliminating the *Konigsberg* as quickly as possible, for on 1 July it was reported that on 1 August three British cruisers, *Hyacinth*, *Pegasus* and *Astrea*, were to call at the island of Zanzibar for coaling. Together, they formed the Royal Navy's Cape Squadron, commanded by Rear Admiral Sir Herbert King-Hall. Individually, they were not impressive, having once formed part of Queen Victoria's navy, added to which they were far slower than the *Konigsberg* and armed with less powerful guns. Nevertheless, working together under a capable commander, they had the capacity to destroy or at least neutralise *Konigsberg*. Looff therefore put to sea on 31 July.

Ten miles out, his masthead lookout reported the presence of three ships. They were clearly King-Hall's cruisers, for as soon as *Konigsberg* came into view they quickly deployed to intercept her as if war had been declared – one remaining ahead, one deploying to port and the third to starboard. Looff reversed course and rang down for maximum speed. Soon the stokehold was filled with the sound of scraping shovels and slamming fire doors as the sweating stokers re-doubled their efforts in the equatorial heat. Anxious engineer officers tapped the brass-cased pressure gauges as the needles crept ever higher towards the danger zone. At length *Konigsberg* reached her maximum speed in excess of 24 knots and the British ships began to fade from view.

Then, luck came to Looff's aid in the form of heavy, driving rain. Unseen by his opponents, he reversed course, sliding past *Astraea*, King-Hall's flagship, without attracting attention and sped away to the south. All that dawn revealed to the British lookouts was a completely empty sea. Such was the Admiral's rage that it remained firmly fixed in the memories of those within earshot.

Looff's escape, however, had been bought at the price of most of his precious coal and he was forced to arrange a rendezvous with the *Somali*. On 4 August *Konigsberg's* radio operator received a coded transmission consisting of the warship's call sign and a single apparently meaningless word which he entered on a message form – egima. He handed the form to the officer of the watch who, because of its high security classification, took it straight to Looff. It was clearly something the captain had been expecting. After glancing briefly at the codeword he remarked that Germany was now at war with Great Britain and the ship's company should be assembled so that he could inform them of the fact.

Shortly after, a Japanese liner was intercepted and boarded. For the moment, Japan was neutral and would not enter the war on the side of the Entente powers until 23 August. As the liner's officers believed the cruiser to be British, polite bewilderment was the order of the day. The boarding party was welcomed with smiles and bows, to which its commander replied with clicked heels and a correct salute. After a comparison of the manifest with the cargo and a search of the ship the Japanese were permitted to go on their way, both sides doubtless wondering what it had all been about. Next, two German freighters, the *Zeithen* and the *Hansa*, ignorant of the outbreak of war, were prevented from entering the Red Sea and making their way to the Suez Canal, where they would certainly have been interned. A third German cargo ship, the *Goldenfels*, made a pointless attempt to avoid what her captain believed to be a British cruiser, and joined the convoy. At length, on 6 August, *Konigsberg* finally halted a British merchantman, the *City of Winchester*. Her holds were filled with general cargo, including the first crop of the Indian tea harvest, but while Looff was hoping to take her coal aboard it was found to be of such poor quality as to be not worth the trouble of handling. After some 400 tons of cargo were transferred to the German freighters they were told to head for East Africa while the British ship was scuttled after providing Looff's gunners with some target practice.

During the next few weeks *Konigsberg* met *Somali* on three occasions without so much as sighting another ship. By the end of August the cruiser's coal bunkers were only one-quarter full and at the suggestion of *Somali's* captain, who had a detailed knowledge of the East African coast, the two ships entered the Rufiji River on 3 September and steamed up the Simba Uranga Channel before making fast. A request for coal and supplies was then despatched to Dar es Salaam. After a while coal lighters began to make their journey along the coast, their contents being sufficient to meet the ships' domestic requirements and leave a little in hand.

Looff had organised a system of coastal lookouts among the local population and on 19 September he was informed that a two-funnel warship had entered Zanzibar harbour. He calculated that the new arrival could only be the *Astraea* or the *Pegasus* and decided to eliminate her at once. *Konigsberg* left the Rufiji on the afternoon tide and by the following morning was approaching Zanzibar harbour. A blank round was fired at the small harbour guard ship, a former German tug named *Helmuth*, which her master wisely interpreted as a signal to stay out of the way. Beyond, Looff was able to identify the *Pegasus* and, satisfied that she was alone, gave the order to open fire at 9,000 yards range. After the first two or three salvos *Konigsberg* was scoring regular hits. His task was made the easier by the fact that the British cruiser was completely immobile, having entered Zanzibar for a much-needed boiler clean and machinery overhaul. Her commander, Captain John Ingles, tried to raise steam and reply in kind, but his eight 4-inch guns were hopelessly outranged by Looff's ten 4.1-inch main armament. The contest was akin to that between a fit middle-weight boxer and a bed-ridden invalid. After twenty minutes, with *Pegasus* on fire and sinking by the bows, Ingles gave the order to abandon ship. Thirty-eight of his men were dead and fifty-five had been wounded. Looff then turned his attention to the *Helmuth*, killing her Indian engineer and causing some damage before turning away. By evening the *Konigsberg* was back in the Rufiji with her crew in understandably high spirits. Among the officers, however, this was somewhat dampened by the discovery of a broken piston rod crosshead in one of the engines. In addition, the boiler required the sort of serious maintenance that could only be supplied by a dockyard. The nearest such facility was in Dar es Salaam, 100 miles distant, and that meant that the boilers had to be dragged there and back on wooden sledges. For the moment, there would be no more forays onto the high seas.

Two days after the *Pegasus* had been sunk by the *Konigsberg*, the *Emden* bombarded Madras. This was altogether too much for the Admiralty in London. Something had to be done to rein in the activities of the German cruisers east of Suez, and done quickly. The cruiser *Chatham* was ordered down from the Red Sea, followed by two more cruisers, *Dartmouth* and *Weymouth*. Any one of these was a match for the *Konigsberg* and together they put an end to Looff's hopes that once again he might take his ship out into open water, even if he could obtain sufficient coal.

Under Captain Drury-Lowe of the *Chatham*, the entire effort of the new arrivals was devoted to finding and destroying the German cruiser. Early in September *Chatham* entered the little port of Lindi in the south of the German colony. Governor Schnee had declared this to be a neutral or at least non-belligerent location. Inside was a German merchantman, the *Prasident*, which, it was claimed, had been converted for use as a hospital ship and was actually flying a red cross flag. A boarding party discovered neither patients nor the means to treat patients, but did discover orders to deliver coal to a location in the Rufiji River. When questioned, members of the crew confirmed that a cargo had already been delivered to a destination in the river but were unable or unwilling to identify it. A modern German chart containing more detailed information than that in the possession of the *Chatham* showed a village named Salale in the delta, but no one seemed to have heard of it.

After disabling the *Präsident's* engines, *Chatham* headed north along the coast. As she approached the small island of Komo, lying off the Rufiji delta, a man in khaki uniform was seen running along the beach and disappearing into a palm grove. This in itself was suspicious and a party was landed to investigate. A German officer was found in a hut that served as a signal station, together with a diary in which the *Königsberg* was mentioned as well as the mysterious Salale. It looked as though the German cruiser's lair had been found, but at this point *Chatham* was called away on a wild goose chase initiated by an agent's false report that *Königsberg* had been sighted in Dar es Salaam harbour, another of Governor Schnee's non-combatant zones. This was simply not true, but some of Drury-Lowe's officers thought that they could see the cruiser's masts inside the harbour, some 6 miles distant. Drury-Lowe hoisted a flag demanding that the German authorities send out a boat and when they did not he opened fire on the town. White flags appeared everywhere and some twenty minutes later a boat appeared, containing some furious German officials. Neither side spoke the other's language and all that was agreed was that *Chatham* should fetch the former British consul at Dar es Salaam from Zanzibar. She returned on 22 October and several naval officers accompanied the party into the harbour where it was confirmed that a floating dock had been sunk in the fairway, blocking it. The Germans angrily pointed out that the British were already aware of the fact. This was perfectly true and was contained in a report written by Lieutenant Turner of the *Pegasus* when the cruiser had visited Dar es Salaam on 8 August. Unfortunately, Turner had been killed when the *Pegasus* was sunk and no one had bothered to read his report. Drury-Lowe was therefore left with a considerable quantity of egg on his face, but the consequences of bombarding the town were far worse. Governor Schnee had hoped to maintain the colony's neutrality so that the reforms he had put in place could take root. Against this, Lettow-Vorbeck, his military commander, took a more realistic view that one cannot remain at peace when a state of war had already been declared. The enraged German population of the colony not only rallied to the latter viewpoint but also declared that similar agreements on local neutrality were null and void.

Just what that meant became apparent on 2 November when a British attempt was made to capture the town of Tanga, in the north of the colony, by means of an amphibious landing. While Drury-Lowe took *Chatham* off to renew the search for *Konigsberg*, the troops detailed to capture Tanga were sailing south from Mombasa in Kenya. Known as Force B, they were drawn from the Indian Army's 27th Bangalore Brigade and an Imperial Service Brigade. With the exception of the 2nd Loyal (North Lancashire) Regiment and a battalion of Kashmir Rifles, they were completely inexperienced, semi-trained and semi-disciplined. Despite this, Force B was 8,000 strong and should have experienced no difficulty in taking the town from the 1,000 men that were all that Lettow-Vorbeck could muster, had it not been for its commander, Major General A.E. Aitken, who committed his troops to the attack without the ability to control them once they were in motion, or detailed planning or any reconnaissance of the enemy's positions. The Royal Navy's gunfire support, provided by the cruiser *Fox*, was distributed between British and German troops and the hospital in which staff were trying to treat the wounded of both sides. Even the local bees, famed for their ferocity and enraged by the destruction of their nests by rifle and machine-gun fire, seemed to have a particular dislike for Force B. The majority of the Indian units fled, leaving the Loyals and the Kashmir Rifles to hold their ground. By 4 November a disorderly embarkation was in progress. Having retired to the beach with their discipline firmly intact, the Loyals were disgusted by an order to leave their machine guns behind. The statistics of the action tell their own story. Force B's casualties amounted to 800 killed, 500 wounded and several hundreds more missing or in enemy hands. Lettow-Vorbeck's losses came to fifteen Europeans and fifty-four askaris killed. Abandoned by Force B were a dozen machine guns, many hundred rifles, 600,000 rounds of ammunition and huge quantities of clothing and blankets. Aitken's court martial saw him stripped of his command, reduced two steps in rank and placed on half-pay for the rest of the war.

The gloves were now definitely off. The era of make-believe neutrality was over and in recognition of the fact, as well as a desire to exact some revenge for the disaster at Tanga, the battleship *Goliath* shelled Dar es Salaam on 28 and 30 November. This caused extensive damage to the town and raised war fever among the population to fever pitch.

Meanwhile, *Chatham* had returned to a position off the Rufiji. A landing party brought back three natives who, in a state of rum-induced euphoria, confirmed that not only were the *Konigsberg* and the *Somali* hiding up the Simba Uranga Channel near a village called Salale, but also that the Germans had covered the approaches with the cruiser's secondary armament and machine guns, concealed among the mangrove swamps. From *Chatham's* masthead a lookout scanned the appropriate bearing and was able to pick out four masts above the tree canopy. *Konigsberg* had been found but it seemed that there was no way of hitting her. At high tide the closest *Chatham* could approach the shoreline was 2 miles. From this position a calculation with the aid of a chart showed that the two ships were 14,800 yards apart, and the maximum range of *Chatham's* guns was 14,500 yards. Not to be beaten, her captain shifted his ballast to produce a list that gave his guns extra elevation and therefore range. He opened fire on 2 November without result. Five days later, however, he hit the *Somali* and set her ablaze. Against this, *Konigsberg* moved further up-river, out of range, and camouflaged her masts.

The question now was what to do next. *Goliath's* 12-inch guns might provide an answer but shallow water kept her even further from the shore than *Chatham*. *Konigsberg* was now even further away and Looff kept changing her position to confuse her attackers. The problems for the latter remained preventing her escape and actually destroying her. The first was partially solved by sinking an old merchantman, the *Newbridge*, across the Simba Uranga Channel with the assistance of the tug *Duplex*.

Given the nature of Looff's defences at the mouths of the delta, the mission was considered suicidal and open only to volunteers. In the event, only two men were killed despite the hail of fire directed at the ships. Dummy mines were also laid off the mouths of the other channels. As for eliminating the German cruiser altogether the suggestion that she should be captured by a cutting-out expedition in the best Nelsonian tradition was quickly discarded. So, too, was the idea of dropping bombs as the bombload carried by the aircraft of the day was unlikely to cause the German crew much more than a noisy inconvenience. It was, however, agreed that aircraft held the key to some aspects of the problem. A Curtiss flying boat was purchased from a South African mining engineer and a civilian pilot, also named Curtis, was hired to fly it, being granted a commission as a Sub-Lieutenant in the Royal Naval Air Service. On 19 November he was able to confirm the *Konigsberg's* current position. Thereafter, move the cruiser wherever he might, Looff was rarely free from the attentions of reconnaissance aircraft. These included two Sopwiths and three Short seaplanes. Unfortunately, most of the aircraft had only a brief operational life as the glue holding the fabric to the frame tended to melt in the humid tropical heat.

On 1 January 1915 *Chatham* was relieved by *Weymouth* and the decision was reached to tow two shallow-draft monitors out from England via the Mediterranean and the Red Sea. On arrival in the Rufiji delta, they would move up the channel and engage the *Konigsberg*, their fire being controlled by wireless aircraft. The problem was that their voyage would take several months. In the meantime, Looff received the following signal from Berlin:

Supply ship is on its way to you. Should arrive before spring tides and will signal her approach by pre-arranged code. Bringing 1,600 tons of bunker coal and rifles munitions supplies for von Lettow. Inform Army Commander. Also convey His Majesty's warm congratulations on his victory at Tanga.

The ship was the 1,600-ton former British freighter *Rubens*, which had been caught in Hamburg on the outbreak of war. Now, she had been given a Danish identity, re-named *Kronberg* and was crewed by Danish-speaking Germans. In command was a very capable young officer, Lieutenant Christiansen. On 19 February he sailed from Hamburg amid gales and intermittent snow and gambled successfully that the British would not expect a blockade runner to pass through the gap between the Shetlands and the Orkneys. *Kronberg* remained undetected during her long passage south through the Atlantic, round the Cape of Good Hope and into the Indian Ocean. At Aldabra Island, approximately 600 miles from the Rufiji delta, Christiansen decided that he must break radio silence and contact Looff regarding *Konigsberg's* anticipated breakout into open water, little knowing of the British blockade waiting outside the river mouth. On Madagascar a French radio station picked up a signal originating in the Mozambique Channel. It consisted of the letters AKO repeated several times. The Allies had been in possession of the German naval code for some time and AKO was known to be the *Konigsberg's* call sign. It followed, therefore, that as the *Konigsberg* was known to be locked up inside the Rufiji delta, the origin of the signal must be a blockade runner trying to contact her.

The information was passed to the Royal Navy and two days later the AKO signal was heard again. It was stronger and therefore its origin was much closer. As Admiral King-Hall was now in overall command of the warships blockading the Rufiji and he reasoned, correctly, that as the blockade runner was unable to reach the *Konigsberg* she would either land her cargo at Tanga or across the beaches of the almost land-locked Manza Bay. He therefore transferred his flag to the *Hyacinth* and set off northwards, keeping out of sight of the coast on which Lettow-Vorbeck had established a chain of lookout stations that either lit signal fires or hoisted flags whenever a British warship was in the offing. He had read Christiansen's mind correctly and at first light on 14 April the *Kronberg* was sighted between *Hyacinth* and the coast. Christiansen had been heading for Tanga but when a warning salvo from *Hyacinth* erupted ahead of his bows he turned away immediately and headed for the shelter of the headland at Manza Bay. *Hyacinth* increased her own speed and was confident of sinking the blockade runner. At this point it began to seem as though Christiansen's luck would hold, for with a bang heard throughout the cruiser, the joint between the piston and connecting rod in *Hyacinth's* starboard engine shattered. *Kronberg* disappeared round the headland, pursued by some very inaccurate gunnery that only scored one hit. When *Hyacinth*, limping along on her port engine, finally rounded the headland, *Kronberg* seemed to be on fire and her crew were heading for the shore in her boats. Christiansen had covered her decks with timber and other combustible materials, but this was only a ruse to suggest that the ship was dying. A boarding party from *Hyacinth* did manage to scramble aboard and reach the bridge, from which charts and other documents were taken, but left hurriedly when they were fired on from the shore. This was silenced when the cruiser opened fire but the impression received by King-Hall from the boarders was that *Kronberg* was a complete wreck. Several more rounds were fired into her waterline and then, having repaired her starboard engine, *Hyacinth* returned to the Rufiji.

Much later, King-Hall was horrified to learn the true state of affairs. Christiansen may not have made contact with *Konigsberg* but in other respects his mission had been successful. The fires aboard the blockade runner were quickly extinguished and, as soon as sufficient labourers could be rounded up, her cargo was unloaded. In addition to the coal, there were two field guns, four machine guns, 1,800 rifles, 1,000 4.1-inch shells for *Konigsberg's* guns, 6,500 miscellaneous artillery shells, a ton of explosives, 200 tents and communications equipment. Some of this was carried to *Konigsberg* by bearers and the rest was sent to Lettow-Vorbeck by railway.

Meanwhile, conditions aboard the *Konigsberg* had begun to deteriorate. Supplies of coal, ammunition and food were running very low. There was also a shortage of medicines with which to treat malaria and other tropical diseases that had broken out among the crew. There must have been those aboard who hoped that with sufficient fuel their ship would be able to break out of the foetid environment of the Rufiji with its plague of insects, crocodiles and water snakes and reach the clean freshness of the open sea. Looff was aware that during the spring high tides he could probably squeeze his ship past the *Newbridge*, but beyond that lay only a battle that he could not hope to win and that would serve no useful purpose. Yet, his solitary light cruiser was tying down an unexpectedly large number of Royal Navy warships and keeping them from duties elsewhere.

Nevertheless, this situation could not be expected to last forever and it did not. The two shallow draft monitors, *Severn* and *Mersey*, completed their long tow in June and prepared for action by bolting on additional armour. A small airstrip was laid out on Mafia Island and this became the base for two Caudron and two Henri Farman aircraft that would spot the monitors' fall of shot for them and transmit corrections.

At 06.45 on 5 July the battle was joined. While the rest of the British ships engaged the German advance posts in the swamp, *Severn*, followed by *Mersey*, entered the delta's Kikunja Channel and opened fire at a range of 10,000 yards. *Konigsberg* did not respond until 07.40 but had the better of the day's fighting because of excellent corrections signalled by the advance posts. A direct hit on *Mersey* knocked out one of her guns and killed eight, including an observer on her conning tower. *Severn* was straddled, her decks being showered with stinking mud and dead fish that attracted little enthusiasm from the ship's cooks. The British corrections from the air achieved less success, only seventy-eight out of 635 rounds being corrected, only three of which scored hits on the German cruiser, the most important knocking out a forward gun.

Leaking from near misses, the monitors retired to effect repairs. No doubt the debriefing involved a certain amount of frank discussion for during the days that followed the apparent failure of the air-spotting was analysed and the technique improved beyond recognition. On 11 July the monitors returned to the attack with Lieutenant Cull piloting the spotting aircraft and Sub-Lieutenant Arnold acting as his observer. At a little before noon the eighth salvo to be fired scored direct hits on the cruiser's forecastle. Hits now followed in regular succession and the *Konigsberg* was shaken by a series of internal explosions. Her return fire dwindled away as one gun after another was silenced and her ammunition was shot off. One of the last rounds to be fired was a shrapnel shell that burst close to Cull's aircraft, tearing loose one of its two engines. Despite losing height steadily Cull managed to keep the aircraft flying while Arnold continued to send corrections until the cruiser was hidden by trees. When, finally, the plane hit the water, Cull was able to swim to the bank but Arnold was drowned. This was the first occasion in history when a warship was destroyed by indirect gunfire controlled from the air and, suitably adapted for fiction, formed an episode in Wilbur Smith's novel *Shout at the Devil*.

By 13.30 fires were raging from end to end aboard *Konigsberg*. Looff, knowing that his ship was doomed, ordered her to be abandoned. Simultaneously, the magazines were flooded and two torpedo heads were placed so as to blow out the keel. At 14.40 these exploded, the cruiser settled into the Rufiji slime and Admiral King-Hall recalled the monitors.

That was not quite the end of *Konigsberg's* story. Thirty-three members of her crew had been killed and more, including Looff, wounded. Despite this, he worked his 188 surviving crewmen hard, manhandling ten 4.1-inch and two 3.5-inch guns ashore and sending them off to the railway workshops in Dar es Salaam where they were fitted with carriages. They were employed in various roles throughout the long East African campaign and provided Lettow-Vorbeck with a weight of fire his opponents could not match; some of them still exist.

Konigsberg was the last of the Imperial German Navy's cruisers to sail the world's high seas. As a commerce raider she had had little success, but for eight months she had held out against heavy odds and had fought to the end. The Kaiser ennobled Looff and promoted him to Captain. This gave him seniority over Lettow-Vorbeck, which he wisely declined to exercise. Captured during the campaign, he was interrogated regarding Zeppelin L.59's aborted flight from Europe to East Africa, causing serious, if temporary, alarm by announcing that the Zeppelins would be used to transport reinforcements to East Africa, each airship being capable of carrying one infantry company. It took his captors a little while to understand that it was they who were being taken for a ride.

After the war ended Lettow-Vorbeck and his troops were permitted to parade through the Brandenburg Gate and were loudly cheered by crowds of Berliners. Looff also took part in the parade, together with fifteen of his old seamen, the last survivors of *Konigsberg's* crew.

CHAPTER 9

Queens of the Lake

If anyone thought that the sinking of the *Konigsberg* ended naval operations in German East Africa, they were gravely mistaken. Four hundred miles inland from the coast was Lake Tanganyika, the longest lake in the world, measuring 400 miles from north to south and 47 miles across at its narrowest point. The lake provided a natural boundary between German territory, the Belgian Congo (Zaire) to the west and Rhodesia (Zimbabwe) to the south. The Germans enjoyed complete control of the lake because since 1914 they had fitted out three armed steamers whereas the British and Belgians had none. Since the disastrous landing at Tanga there had been no further attempts to invade the German colony and any attempt to do so from the west or south was, for the moment, out of the question because the enemy would promptly threaten the Allied rear with an amphibious landing wherever he chose.

An indefinite stalemate on the lake seemed quite probable until, in April 1915, a big game hunter named John Lee requested and was granted an interview with Admiral Sir Henry Jackson, the First Sea Lord. Lee was familiar with every aspect of central Africa and he was seriously concerned that Lettow-Vorbeck's raiding activities might provoke tribal uprisings in Rhodesia and the Congo. He knew that the German flotilla on the lake presented Allied commanders with a serious headache, but he was able to offer a solution to the problem. This involved shipping out an armed motor boat that could sink the enemy's warships. It was almost certainly in Jackson's mind to have Lee politely shown the door, but the latter forestalled him by unrolling a detailed map of the Congo.

First, Lee's finger traced a railway line 175 miles long joining Kabalo with Lukuga on the western shore of the lake. Of course, getting the motor boat to Kabalo would involve shipping it by rail from South Africa to the Congo, then a difficult overland journey that would require the assistance of steam traction engines, teams of oxen and hundreds of native labourers. Lee confirmed that he had travelled the entire route and believed that it offered a real possibility of getting at the Germans. Jackson was sufficiently interested to take the opinions of the War and Colonial Offices, both of whom confirmed Lee's view. No better idea of dealing with the enemy on Lake Tanganyika had been forthcoming and Jackson, now converted to it, decided to carry it through with the purchase of two petrol-driven mahogany motor boats, capable of 15 knots. These were each fitted with a 3-pounder gun on the foredeck and a Maxim machine gun aft.

John Lee, given the rank of lieutenant commander in the Royal Naval Volunteer Reserve, was permitted to accompany the expedition as its Second-in-Command. The problem now was to find a suitable officer to command it. Of those officers of appropriate rank available, none wished to become involved in an apparently suicidal venture which, at best, would turn out to be nothing more than a fool's errand – with one exception. His name was Geoffrey Basil Spicer-Simson and he was the oldest lieutenant commander in the Royal Navy, claiming, with some justice, that he had been repeatedly passed over for promotion. His early service took place aboard China gunboats and he had carried out a survey of the Gambia River in West Africa, but his career was marred not only by the ramming and sinking of a liberty boat but also by a very unfortunate manner. He was autocratic, overbearing, unpredictable, opinionated, knowledgeable on every subject under the sun, eccentric and vain, none of which increased his popularity. Nor did the fact that his trunk and limbs were tattooed with snakes, nor his use of a cigarette holder, which was considered to be a trifle effeminate in a naval officer. On the outbreak of war he was appointed commander of the Downs Boarding Flotilla, consisting of two elderly torpedo gunboats, the precursors of the modern destroyer, and six armed tugs. This phase of his career ended a fortnight later when, having ordered the gunboat *Niger* to anchor east of the Deal Bank Buoy, he disappeared to entertain some ladies in a hotel. Unfortunately, a prowling U-boat took advantage of the stationary target to torpedo and sink it. In the circumstances it was no surprise that the Admiralty should decide that he would be better employed manning a desk in its Personnel Department. Equally, it accepted with pleasure his offer to command the Lake Tanganyika expedition, believing that the risk of losing Lieutenant Commander Spicer-Simson was probably justified. He immediately enraged Their Lordships by announcing that he would call his motor boats *Dog* and *Cat* and was ordered to choose other names. In the event, they went to war as *Mimi* and *Toutou*. After carrying out trials on the Thames the expedition, consisting of four officers and twenty-four ratings, sailed for Cape Town from Tilbury aboard the Union Castle Line's *Llanstephan Castle* on 11 June 1915. Also aboard, for quite different reasons, was the Astronomer Royal, who was forced to sit in open-mouthed astonishment while Spicer-Simson lectured him on the constellations of the Southern Hemisphere.

At Cape Town the boats were lifted on to railway flats and the party began an apparently endless journey by train on 2 July. Some 2,700 miles later they reached Fungurume in the Congo, where they found Lee waiting for them. He had left England some time ahead of them to make arrangements for the next and most difficult phase of the journey through 120 miles of bush. The boats would be carried on trailers made from the fore carriages of ox wagons, which were capable of the hardest usage. Some 50 tons of supplies had to be loaded into wagons that were hauled by over forty oxen. Large numbers of natives were hired as drivers, cooks and general labourers. Not least, a quantity of tools had to be assembled as Lee knew that in places the track ahead would need strengthening and widening while bridges and culverts needed strengthening to cope with the weight that would be imposed on them. On 14 August the railway delivered two steam traction engines. These were checked over and four days later the column set off. Hard physical work, heat, insects, dust and water shortage made the journey anything but pleasant. Once again, it was Lee's foresight that kept the expedition moving. Without water for their boilers the traction engines could not be used, so he recruited large numbers of native women to carry pots on their heads from the nearest water source, which could be as far as 8 miles away. Six weeks after leaving Fungurume the column reached Sankisia having negotiated bush, forest and a mountain range.

At Sankisia the boats and supplies were transferred to the flats of a narrow gauge railway. The line only ran to Bukama on the Lualaba River, just 15 miles distant, where everything had to be off-loaded again. The sense of anti-climax must have been enormous and probably generated a shortness of temper. Whatever, Spicer-Simson had a row with Lee, without whom he would not have got this far, and gracelessly sent him packing.

However, the worst of the journey lay behind the expedition. From Bukama its route took it 200 miles along the river to Kabalo, from whence a railway ran the last 175 miles to Lukuga on the western shore of Lake Tanganyika. The principal difficulty lay in the fact that at this time of year there was little depth of water in the river. However, Jack Tar has always been a man of considerable ingenuity and the two motor boats were floated by lashing empty casks to their keels, thereby increasing their buoyancy. Even so, there were places where the water was so shallow that the boats had to be manhandled. Simultaneously, the supplies were loaded into canoes and anything else that would float and propelled downstream by teams of native paddlers. At Kabalo trans-shipment was completed for the last time and on 28 October the expedition's train steamed into Lukuga.

Naturally the Belgians were delighted by the expedition's arrival. Many of them had received no news from home for well over a year and were grateful for anything that the sailors could tell them. They were more than a little startled by Spicer-Simson's version of shirt-sleeve order in which his shorts were replaced by a skirt, while the natives were deeply awed by the tattooed snakes on his thighs and forearms.

Regarding the German flotilla on the lake, the Belgians were able to supply much useful information. The largest was the *Graf von Gotzen*, named after the former governor of the colony. She was said to be armed with at least one 4.1-inch and two smaller guns salvaged from the wreck of the *Konigsberg*, but her maximum speed was limited to six knots. The *Hedwig von Wissmann* could reach ten knots but was much smaller, mounting two 6-pounder guns forward and one 37mm Hotchkiss aft. The smallest of the three was the *Kingani*, capable of seven knots but armed with only a single 37mm Hotchkiss forward. The flotilla was based at Kigoma on the opposite shore of the lake, to the north. It was under the command of Lieutenant Commander Gustav von Zimmer who, thanks to Central African gossip, had been informed of the expedition's approach. His view was that such an undertaking was physically impossible and that the rumours were preposterous and should be ignored.

Spicer-Simson's first task was to secure his base. He was aware that the lake was subject to sudden, violent storms that could wreck his frail boats. The Belgians were asked to build a breakwater, which they did by blasting rock from the nearby cliffs. By late December the newly formed harbour, named Kalemie, was ready for use. On Christmas Eve *Mimi* and *Toutou* were launched and completed their trials satisfactorily. Christmas Day was spent in the traditional manner, but on 26 December the Belgians reported a steamer moving down the lake from the north. As the distance closed, the image hardened into the *Kingani*, engaged in a routine examination of the Belgian fortifications at Lukuga.

Spicer-Simson let her pass, then followed at a distance with *Mimi* and *Toutou*, widely separated so that the enemy would have to split his fire between them. A sudden belch of smoke from *Kigani's* funnel and a steady turn to port indicated that she was simultaneously trying to escape and bring her gun into action. At 2,000 yards the motor boats opened fire. Immediately, their crews made the unwelcome discovery that unless their 3-pounders were fired directly ahead their recoil could cause damage to their flimsy hulls. Coupled with the need to dodge the German fire, this meant that at first their rate of fire was limited to about one round per minute. *Kigani* was engaging *Toutou* with her 37mm gun and firing small arms at *Mimi*, without hitting either. The advantages of speed and firepower possessed by the British boats now began to tell. With the range down to 1,100 yards, *Mimi* slammed a shell through the enemy's gunshield, killing the ship's captain and two petty officers. When another round killed the warrant officer who had attempted to take command, *Kigani's* native crew began jumping overboard and swimming for the shore. The ship's chief engineer then emerged and hauled down the German colours. *Toutou* came alongside to escort the prize into Kalemie where, taking in water rapidly from a shell hole in her port bunker, she was beached in just sufficient time to prevent her sinking.

It was unfortunate that Spicer-Simson chose this particular moment to boast openly to his men about his prowess as a gunnery expert, for it had been the 3-pounder gun layers who deserved all the credit, such corrections as he had given being drowned out by the roar of the Thornycroft engine. This was bad enough as they had little enough liking for him anyway, but he could hardly have avoided the contempt in their eyes when he took an ornate gold ring from the finger of the dead German captain and slipped it on his own.

Having been patched up and made watertight, *Kingani* was given the new name of *Fifi* and suitably rearmed. The Belgians contributed a 12-pounder gun from one of their coast defence batteries and this was mounted forward while the blind spot aft was closed with a spare 3-pounder. On 14 January 1916 one of the lake's periodic storms swept down its length, battering *Toutou* against the breakwater and causing sufficient damage for her to remain out of commission for a while. *Fifi* began dragging her anchor but good seamanship got her clear of the harbour and, having put out a sea-anchor, she managed to ride out the gale.

Shortly after dawn on 9 February the Belgian lookouts reported *Hedwig von Wissmann* coming down the lake. The day's heat was building up when Spicer-Simson boarded *Fifi* and immediately set off to intercept her, accompanied by Lieutenant A.E. Wainwright in *Mimi*. The Germans believed that the former *Kingani* had been sunk by Belgian coast defence batteries and were looking for some evidence to support the theory. Heat haze and thermals above the flat surface of the water prevented the German captain, Lieutenant Odebrecht, from seeing his opponents until they were only 4 miles distant. He immediately reversed course and headed for Kigoma.

The funnels of both steamers began to pour black smoke as oil-soaked wood balks were flung into their furnaces to raise boiler pressure quickly. Wainwright, taking full advantage of *Mimi's* speed, forged ahead, opening fire at 3,000 yards range, beyond which the enemy's stern-mounted 37mm gun could not reply. This seems to have produced results, for Odebrecht began making a series of short turns to starboard to bring his forward 6-pounders into action. Whenever this happened, Wainwright turned to starboard and the enemy shells burst in empty space. These brief pauses enabled *Fifi* to catch up. Wainwright drew alongside and shouted to Spicer-Simson that his 12-pounder shells were falling well ahead of the enemy. No doubt the seamen concealed their pleasure that their resident gunnery expert had been found wanting by a junior reserve officer, but the appropriate correction was made and the 12-pounder's next round produced dramatic results. It punched a hole into the enemy's hull to explode in his engine room and blew a hole in her side. Burning fiercely, her steering gear wrecked and her engines stopped, *Hedwig von Wissmann* fell away to starboard in a sinking condition and fifteen minutes later disappeared below the surface of the lake. Odebrecht, fifteen Germans and eight native crewmen were rescued from the water.

It would have been quite natural for Zimmer to wonder what had happened to the rest of his flotilla. When, the following day, *Graf von Gotzen* came down the lake, the British crews were confident that they could deal with her, despite her much larger size. Inexplicably, Spicer-Simson stubbornly refused to leave the harbour although repeatedly urged to do so by his officers. No reason was offered for his decision and the German ship was permitted to retreat back over the horizon. Not for the last time, the British officers and men felt that their commander had brought shame on them.

As the balance of power on the lake had now shifted in favour of the Allies, it was decided to commence land operations against German

East Africa. The British invaded from Kenya in the north and Rhodesia in the south while the Belgians invaded from the north-west. Spicer-Simson, now promoted to commander, a recipient both of the Distinguished Service Order and the Belgian *Croix de Guerre* with Three Palms, was ordered to ferry stores north to Tongwe where the Belgians were constructing a seaplane base. From this a number of air attacks were mounted on the *Graf von Gotzen* which, it was claimed, had sustained bomb damage. Whatever the truth, Zimmer scuttled her outside Kigoma harbour.

In the meantime, Spicer-Simson had been ordered to take his flotilla south to Kituta in Rhodesia and support operations to capture the German base of Bismarcksburg, with the specific task of ensuring that the enemy garrison did not escape by means of the lake. On 5 June his three craft arrived off the enemy port but were unable to make contact with any of the Rhodesian troops. On the other hand, inside the harbour there were five dhows that the German regularly used to transport their troops. They were a sitting target but Spicer-Simson refused to open fire on them, nor would he permit his officers to do so on the grounds that this would bring their craft within range of the guns in the whitewashed fort overlooking the harbour. The flotilla withdrew to Kituta and did not return to Bismarcksburg until 9 June, the day before Spicer-Simson believed that the Rhodesians would reach the area. To his horror, he found that the Germans had gone, as had the dhows, and it was the Union Flag that now flew above the fort. On entering the harbour the flotilla was met by an infantry officer who clearly had little respect for Spicer-Simson. Why, he wanted to know, had he permitted the Germans to escape the previous night when the Rhodesians had them boxed in the landward? Obviously, no reasonable explanation could be offered and Spicer-Simson was told to report to a Colonel Murray in the fort. Unwisely, the Commander chose not to change out of his skirt so that when he entered the courtyard he was subjected laughter and yells of derision from the Rhodesian infantrymen relaxing in the shade. No one knows what passed between Murray and Spicer-Simson but the latter emerged from the discussion ashen and incoherent.

After this, his actions became so erratic that the expedition's medical officer recommended that he should be sent home on the grounds of nervous debility, which covered a multitude of sins. Following his treatment, he returned to his desk at the Admiralty, still sporting the ring he had taken from the dead German captain. In due course he received prize money for the capture of the *Kingani* and some smaller craft, as well as head money, based on the number of enemy casualties inflicted. Yet more money resulted from press interviews and lectures in which a very different gloss was put on the *Graf von Gotzen* and Bismarcksburg episodes. Finally, he had his portrait painted in naval full dress, including a cocked hat. Despite his unfortunate personality, these rewards should not be begrudged him as he had successfully executed a mission many of his peers thought impossible, without losing a man. Yet John Lee, the architect of the mission, received nothing.

The story inspired the author C.S. Forester to write his novel *The African Queen*, which became a film of the same name. Two of the original story's participants survived the war. *Toutou* was despatched by rail to Cape Town where she was installed at Victoria Docks having received a wash and brush up and a polished plate inscribed as follows: 'This launch served in the East African Campaign as an armed cruiser. Captured and sank two German gunboats with the assistance of sister launch *Mimi*.' Before the Germans scuttled *Graf von Gotzen* outside Kigoma harbour they applied a thick coating of grease to her machinery, clearly intending that one day she should be raised and taken back into service. That day came in 1924 when she was raised by a Royal Navy salvage team. Disarmed, restored, renamed *Liemba* and given a slightly more modern appearance, she plied the lake until 2010 when she was finally withdrawn after a century of service.

CHAPTER 10

The End of the Greyhounds

It was Kaiser Wilhelm II's ambition that Imperial Germany should not only be a major naval power but also project her greatness in maritime affairs at sea with a range of fast, luxurious liners that would rival those of Great Britain for speed and comfort and even wrest from her the coveted Blue Ribands, awarded for the fastest eastbound and westbound crossings of the Atlantic Ocean.

The first of the new liners, *Kaiser Wilhelm der Grosse*, was launched in 1897. She had beautiful lines and was the first ocean liner to carry four funnels, arranged in two pairs of two. In addition, she was the first to be fitted with watertight bulkhead doors linked to an indicator board on the bridge, the first to be equipped with a Marconi radio transceiver, and the first to win the Blue Riband for the fastest trans-Atlantic run for forty years, completed at a sustained speed 22.3 knots. All in all, it was no surprise that she was known as the *Wundershiff* (Wonder Ship)

Kaiser Wilhelm der Grosse, usually referred to simply as *KWdG*, was built at the AG Vulcan shipyard in Stettin, as were her sister ships *Kronprinz Wilhelm*, *Kaiser Wilhelm II* and *Kronprinzessin Cecilie*. Passengers aboard them would have noticed a number of unusual metal fittings along the deck which were the mountings for the guns that would be installed in time of war, thereby converting the ships to armed merchant cruisers. Along the New York waterfront they were known collectively as the Hohenzollerns of Hoboken, references to the name of Germany's Imperial family and the location of Norddeutscher Lloyd's berth at New Jersey. In 1900 she managed to escape a serious fire on the pier that claimed numerous lives on nearby ships. Her luck continued until 1906, when a gash over 80 feet long was ripped in her hull following a high speed collision with the steamer *Orinoco's* bow, killing five of her sleeping passengers. By 1913 the number of First and Second Class passengers was declining while the number of emigrants was rising. The ship was also beginning to show signs of wear and she was therefore modified to provide accommodation for Third and Steerage Class passengers only.

The *Kaiser Wilhelm der Grosse* was in Bremen when war broke out the following year. She received her guns and naval crew on 4 August and, under the command of Captain Max Reymann, broke out into the Atlantic, keeping as far north as possible to avoid the British blockade. On 7 August, to the south of Iceland, she stopped and sank an insignificant fishing vessel, the *Tubal Cain*, displacing only 227 tons. Her orders then required her to head south and prey on the busy shipping lane off the west coast of Africa. On 15 August she stopped the liner *Galician*, belonging to the Union Castle Line, south of Tenerife. A boarding party carried out the customary search but nothing happened for several hours, during which it seems Reymann was thinking over what to do with his prize. At the end of this he signalled *Galician*: 'I will not destroy you as you have women and children aboard – Good Bye.' The following day she sank two ships, the *Kaipara* of 7,392 tons, and the smaller *Nyanga* of 3,066 tons. By now the folly of using ocean greyhounds as armed merchant cruisers was becoming apparent, for the level of coal in *KWdG's* bunkers was dropping at an alarming rate. Arrangements were made for her to rendezvous with two colliers, *Arucas* and *Duala*, at Rio de Oro on the coast of West Africa. The problem was that Rio de Oro was a Spanish colony and the proposed coaling would take place in Spanish territorial waters.

The disappearance of the *Kaipara* and *Nyanga* had caused some concern in shipping circles. The Royal Navy had detailed two cruisers, the *Vindictive* and the *Highflyer*, to patrol the sea lanes around the Canary Islands, another Spanish colony. On 26 August *Highflyer*, under the command of Captain Henry Buller, was approaching Rio de Oro.

Launched in 1900, she was still a handsome ship, her two two tall masts crossed with not one but two yards and numerous ventilators along her deck combining to give her a distinctive appearance. While she was rapidly becoming obsolescent, her armament, consisting of eleven 6-inch and nine 12-pounder guns, was quite adequate enough to deal with the *Kaiser Wilhelm der Gross,* which mounted only six 4.1-inch guns.

While still some miles from the German raider, Buller could see that she was coaling and clearly in no position to fight. He sent her a signal asking if she surrendered. Reymann answered, somewhat pompously, 'Germans never surrender and you must respect the neutrality of Spain.' The last was a piece of cheek as he had been present for far longer than the twenty-four hours permitted to a ship of war. Unperturbed, Buller replied that he would be back in thirty minutes and that Reymann should use that time to remove the civilian colliers out of the danger area and get his ship ready to fight. Reymann was well aware which way the fight would go and transferred most of those aboard to the two colliers, including the crews of the sunken merchant vessels and those of his crew who were not required to fight and sail the ship.

When a half hour had passed Buller again signalled his opponent to enquire whether he now wished to surrender. Reymann's response was that there was nothing more to discuss. At a little under 10,000 yards Buller ordered one of his 6-pounders to fire a ranging shot. The resulting splash showed that it had fallen short. Reymann replied at once and although his guns threw a lesser weight of metal they were more modern and had a longer range. The result was that *Highflyer* was quickly straddled and began to absorb hits. One exploded against the bridge shortly after Buller had left it for the conning tower. A searchlight was then blasted overboard. An explosion against the superstructure sent a shower of shell splinters into the back of a nearby seaman, the position of the strike clearly indicating that the round had passed between his legs.

Once *Highflyer* was within range the situation changed dramatically. A 4.1-inch gun was shot off the poop and a second round exploded below, starting a major fire. A third round, striking amidships, blew a huge hole in the ship's waterline. Thereafter, *Kaiser Wilhelm der Grosse* received a constant blizzard of 6-pounder shells. In less than thirty minutes the liner's guns had been silenced. As she slowed to a standstill and began list to port three boats were seen pulling for the shore.

Buller ordered *Highflyer* to cease firing and sent his surgeon and sick berth attendants across to the stricken ship with medical supplies to treat those wounded who had remained aboard. From them it was estimated that the enemy's loss amounted to 200 killed and wounded. This was almost certainly too high, but more accurate figures could not be obtained as the ship was listing ever more heavily and the medical party were lucky to get off before she rolled over and sank in 50 feet of water. For her part, *Highflyer* had been hit fifteen times without being seriously damaged and her casualties amounted to one man killed and five slightly wounded.

Reymann's account of his ship's end differs and is somewhat grudging. She ceased firing, he claimed, because she had run out of ammunition. This is a little difficult to believe as she was at the start of her cruise and the action itself barely lasted half an hour. He also suggested that she sank because of demolition charges that he had rigged with a view to scuttling. Again, that seems unlikely as no further explosions were heard aboard her once she had ceased firing and her fatal list was to port, where a gap 60 feet across had been blown in her waterline. Reymann himself reached the shore with the surviving members of his crew that had fought the ship. He then achieved the remarkable feat of returning to Germany on a neutral ship, working his passage as a stoker under an assumed name. Those who escaped the action aboard the colliers were either captured or released, according to their personal circumstances, two weeks later when the Hamburg-Amerika liner *Bethania* was intercepted while trying to run the British blockade.

This action was the first naval duel of the war. It was not a good beginning, for two more of Germany's ocean greyhounds had already been removed from the board. *Kronprinzessin Cecilie* had left New York bound for Bremen when war broke out. Her master, unwilling to take the risks involved in trying to run the British blockade, decided to return to American waters and entered Bar Harbor, Maine, on 4 August. She was ultimately interned and taken into American service as a troop transport when the United States declared war on Germany in 1917. *Kaiser Wilhelm II* had left Bremerhaven for New York on 3 August and, using her speed to evade British cruisers, arrived at her destination three days later. She, too, was subsequently interned and later entered American service.

The fourth, and most successful, of Germany's ocean greyhound sisterhood was the *Kronprinz Wilhelm,* another winner of the Blue Riband. In the palmy days of peace she had been a favourite of those Trans-Atlantic travellers who were involved in the international world of musical entertainment, notably the theatrical and opera producer Oscar Hammerstein, and on one occasion she had conveyed the Kaiser's brother, Crown Prince Albert von Preussen, on a state visit to New York, where he was met by President Theodore Roosevelt. We last came across her in an earlier chapter receiving her armament and naval personnel from the cruiser *Karlsruhe,* from whom she was forced to separate when they were surprised by Admiral Cradock's flagship *Suffolk.* Following this meeting, *Kronprinz Wilhelm* was commanded by Lieutenant Commander Paul Thierfelder, the *Karlsruhe's* navigation officer, with the liner's original skipper as his First Lieutenant.

Having separated from *Karlsruhe,* Thierfelder took *Kronprinz Wilhelm* on an unpredictable course towards the Azores, where he met the collier *Walhalla* and replenished his bunkers. He then headed south-east to the Canary Islands where the German representative informed him that there was no prospect of his being able to obtain further supplies of coal in the area. Thierfelder therefore decided to head for the South American Coast, where there was considerable support for Germany. In addition, he could also top up his supplies from captured ships and seek internment in a neutral port if he found himself unable to proceed further. At this stage, he was unaware that around the entire coast of South America, German naval officers, diplomatic representatives and consular officials were setting up the *Etappendienst,* buying up local coal supplies and chartering ships to convey it to secret rendezvous points at sea, thereby keeping their commerce raiders supplied and active.

Many of the liner's crew were discharged reservists or civilian volunteers and the voyage west was used to get them used to modern Navy ways and train them in various aspects of their duties. In addition, the guns had to be securely mounted and a gunnery practice programme begun. On 3 September a rendezvous was made with the *Karlsruhe's* tender, the collier *Assuncion*, off Rocas Reef. At 20.30 on 4 September a British liner, the *Indian Prince*, hove into view and, having spotted the *Kronprinz Wilhelm's* guns and naval ensign, stopped without the need to have a shot fired across her bows. As a heavy sea was running, Thierfelder's boarding party was unable to scramble aboard her until early the following morning. They found that most of her cargo was of value to the British war effort and that being the case, she would, therefore, have to be sunk. In the meantime, provisions, coal and much else would be of use to the raider, although the transfer of these took a over a period of several days because of the sea conditions. The *Indian Prince's* crew and passengers were brought across during the afternoon of 8 September. The following morning the bottom was blown out of the ship with scuttling charges and Thierfelder, having been informed that the *Etappendienst* was now operating, headed south to a rendezvous with several of its supply ships.

On 14 September Thierfelder made the most serious mistake of his career. As *Kronprinz Wilhelm* was approaching Trinidade Island, off which she was to meet several German ships including another armed merchant cruiser, the *Cap Trafalgar*, the sound of heavy gunfire came rolling across the water. The source of this was, of course, *Cap Trafalgar's* fight to the death with *Carmania*, but Thierfelder was not to know that. Nor could he have known that, when the gunfire ceased, *Carmania* had emerged the victor but was so badly damaged that she could not have survived another such fiercely fought contest with his own ship. Suspecting some sort of trap he turned away and began a successful search for the supply ships he had been promised.

Kronprinz Wilhelm had no further contact with Allied shipping until 7 October when the halted the British steamer *La Correntina*, loaded with frozen meat, off the Brazilian coast. Because of poor weather, it took 14 October to complete the transfer of provisions, coal, passengers and crew from the prize. Also taken from *La Correntina* were two 4.7-inch guns and their shields. They lacked ammunition but were mounted on the *Kronprinz Wilhelm's* poop and used for gun drill, although some of her own ammunition was modified to fire blank cartridges as warning shots. *La Correntina* was then scuttled, although Thierfelder decided to remain in the area because a radio message informed him that her sister ship had left Monte Video on 12 October and entered the same shipping lane. In the event his wait was in vain and he moved off in search of other victims.

Thierfelder had his own thought on how a raider's war should be conducted. He avoided areas where he might run into trouble and preferred to use guile rather than force. He would, for example, assume the same course as an unsuspecting merchantman. Neither freighters nor sailing ships could hope to equal the liner's speed and would expect to be overhauled without attracting suspicion. During this period those aboard the *Kronprinz Wilhelm* did nothing to attract suspicion. Only when she was running parallel would Thierfelder break out his colours and instruct his victim to stop. No one argued and his guns remained a silent but potent threat. Alternatively, he would remain stationary and transmit distress signals so that his intended prey came to him. The boarding party would examine the cargo for commodities that would be of military use to the Allies and if there were none the ship would be released; if not, she would be scuttled after her coal, provisions, crew, passengers and their luggage had been transferred. Operating off the coast of Brazil or Argentina, the *Kaiser Wilhelm II* made a total of sixteen captures during her career as a raider and did so, moreover, without the loss of a single life. Ten of these were British, four were French, one was Norwegian and one was Russian. The Norwegian, a barque named *Semantha*, was, of course, neutral, but she was carrying contraband cargo bound for an Allied port and that ensured her destruction. The Russian schooner *Pittan* obviously belonged to a combatant nation and was fair game but she was apparently of no interest and Thierfelder released her. Altogether, no less than five of the captures were sailing vessels, which illustrates how much of the world's cargo still travelled in this way.

After a while, the *Kaiser Wilhelm II* earned herself such a reputation along the eastern seaboard of South America that fictional accounts of her adventures appeared in the Allied press. These were read with great interest by her crew who learned that she had been sunk in a variety of ways as well as being interned. Other aspects of life aboard were less amusing. Overcrowding had become so bad that Thierfelder sent his reluctant passengers into a neutral port aboard his last capture. A monotonous diet lacking fruit and fresh vegetables was undermining the crew's health to the extent that symptoms of scurvy had begun to appear.

Regular contact was made with German supply ships in rendezvous points in the vastness of the southern Atlantic, although these became less frequent as the voyage progressed. This ultimately brought the raider's career to an end. During the morning of 28 March 1915 she arrived at the rendezvous point to find herself alone. She remained there all day and during the evening her lookouts spotted the distant shapes of two British cruisers escorting a cargo vessel. They passed out of sight without anyone suspecting that the freighter was their supply ship, the *Macedonia*, which had just been captured. Thierfelder waited in vain for several days and finally reached the reluctant conclusion that his supplies of coal and provisions had sunk so low that he could no longer remain operational. He sailed for the east coast of the United States and on 11 April took on a somewhat surprised pilot off Cape Henry. She was directed to a point off Newport News where, with great sadness, Thierfelder rang down *Finished With Engines*. They had driven *Kronprinz Wilhelm* over 37,600 miles during her cruise, in which she had sunk 56,000 tons of Allied shipping. She remained laid up at Norfolk Navy Yard and her crew were held in an internment camp nearby. When the United States declared war on Germany in 1917 she was taken over by the US Navy, renamed *Von Steuben* and served for the rest of the war as a troop transport.

In the internment camp the new arrivals met the crew of the *Prinz Eitel Friedrich,* which, if not quite in the ocean greyhound class, was still a respectable liner of 8,797 tons displacement, originally belonging to the Norddeutscher Lloyd Steamship Company. It will be recalled that she had been converted to the role of armed merchant cruiser at Tsingtao, being provided with the crews and armament of the gunboats of *Luchs* and *Tiger*, a total of four 4.1-inch guns and six 88mm guns. Under Lieutenant Commander Thierichens she had crossed the Pacific with Admiral Graf von Spee's East Asia Squadron, but had neither taken part in the Battle of Coronel nor accompanied Spee's squadron in its disastrous attempt to attack the Falkland Islands. Instead, when Spee departed, she had remained off the west coast of South America, taking her first prize on 5 December 1914.

It was naturally a severe shock to learn some days later that, with the exception of *Dresden*, the East Asia Squadron had been destroyed. Although *Dresden* was known to have escaped to the east coast, it was believed that she was being hunted by several British cruisers. In the circumstances, therefore, any attempt to contact or cooperate with her could be counter-productive for both ships. Sensibly, Thierichens decided to avoid the coast altogether and head west to Easter Island. On 11 December he picked up the French barque *Jean* which, usefully, was loaded with coal, followed by the smaller *Kidalton* next day.

After that, six weeks were to pass before he saw another Allied vessel. He used his time at Easter Island to decide on the best course of action. Little support could be expected if he remained in the Pacific, which was now dominated by the ships of four Allied navies. On the other hand, he was commanding a ship of war and was expected to make the best contribution possible to his country's war effort. By rounding the Horn far to its south and so avoiding any contact with British ships operating from the Falkland Islands he could enter the Atlantic, raid his way northwards and attempt to reach Germany by breaking through the British blockade of the North Sea.

It was after New Year when *Prinz Eitel Friedrich* set off to round the Horn, a dangerous passage that she completed without incident. During the next two months she captured and sank eight more prizes as she headed north. As usual, coal and anything useful as well as crews and passengers were transferred before they were sunk. Thierichens does not seem to have used any of his captures to land civilians in a neutral port, but this did not produce excessive over crowding aboard as the average displacement of the prizes was about 3,000 tons, the largest being the 6,629-ton *Floride*. The crews of ships of this size were usually small and relatively few of them carried passengers.

Thierichens received support from the *Etappendienst's* supply ships while running off the Argentine and Brazilian coasts, but north of the Equator there were very few friends to be found, as Thierfelder was also to discover. With fuel running critically low it was apparent that the ship was not going to reach the North Sea, let alone Germany. On 15 March Thierichens took her into Newport News, where the authorities promptly enforced their obligations as neutrals. These limited not only the time that a warship could remain in the harbour, but also the extent that she could replenish her supplies. What settled *Eitel Friedrich's* fate once and for all was the arrival of two British cruisers, *Cumberland* and *Niobe*, which began prowling the approaches to the harbour just beyond the limit of American territorial waters. Thierichens was well aware that long usage had reduced the builder's stated maximum speed of 17 knots and that he was very seriously out-gunned. He could neither flee nor fight and in the circumstances he had no alternative other than to request internment, which was granted. There the *Eitel Friedrich's* career might have ended had not the United States declared war on Germany in 1917 and taken her back into service as the troop transport *De Kalb*.

CHAPTER 11

Following On

The loss of the entire overseas cruiser fleet by the spring of 1915 was a serious blow to German naval morale, even if it was predictable. Nevertheless, lessons had been learned and these were put into effect. It was appreciated that in the long term U-boats had the capacity to sink a greater tonnage of Allied shipping than had surface raiders, but their activities were restricted to the North Sea, the English Channel and the Western Approaches to the British Isles. There was a strong desire to sink Allied, and particularly British, shipping around the world which, apart from the physical damage inflicted on the enemy's war effort, would reduce confidence in the Royal Navy's ability to protect trade. This could only be done with surface raiders, but the idea of converting fast passenger liners to the role had proved to be a waste of resources in the early days of the war as they consumed huge quantities of coal and could not be supplied for long while they were at sea. The Admiralty was, in fact, proposing a *guerre de course*, which would require adopting the methods of the old privateers. Large vessels bristling with guns would simply scare off any potential victim. What was needed was a number of small, harmless looking vessels with just sufficient speed to overtake the average cargo ship and an armament consisting of concealed guns and torpedo tubes below the water line. In addition, the ability to conceal the raider's true identity with easily erected dummy funnels and masts, different paintwork and foreign flags could be put to good use, although it was not universally applied.

The first of the new raiders was the *Meteor*, displacing only 1,912 tons and resembling any one of thousands of small cargo steamers plying the world's oceans with her raised forecastle, poop and midships superstructure, single funnel and masts with cargo derricks over the fore and aft holds. She had originally been a British packet steamer, the *Vienna*, but had been caught in Hamburg on the outbreak of war. She was taken over by the German Navy and fitted out as a minelayer as well as being armed with two 88mm guns, one 52mm gun and two torpedo tubes. Towards the end of May 1915 she set out on her first voyage under Lieutenant Commander von Knorr. This took her into the White Sea and the approaches to Archangel, where she laid a minefield. On 7 June this accounted for three Russian ships with a total displacement of 10,800 tons. On the way home she sank one Swedish and one Norwegian freighter carrying contraband and made a prize of a second Swedish ship.

Her second voyage was to the Moray Firth on the Scottish coast, where she laid another minefield. The destroyer HMS *Lynx* struck one of the mines while two minesweepers, *Lilac* and *Dahlia*, sustained serious damage while sweeping it.

On her way back to Germany *Meteor* encountered and sank a Norwegian schooner, the *Jason*, on 8 August. Shortly after, she was ordered to stop by a British armed boarding vessel, *The Ramsey*, which closed in so that her boarding party could cross. Prior to being taken up by the Royal Navy *The Ramsey* had ferried holiday crowds in their striped blazers, boaters and parasols from Liverpool to the Isle of Man during the last golden summers before the outbreak of war. Now, understandably, her captain felt that he had nothing to fear from the small, nondescript freighter flying the Russian flag and the atmosphere aboard his ship was relaxed. Suddenly, the Russian flag came down and up went the German naval ensign. Shells from unmasked guns began to smash into the boarding vessel and a torpedo blew off her stern. Within four minutes of the *Meteor* opening fire, *The Ramsey* had gone down, leaving only a pall of smoke hanging over her wreckage. Her captain and fifty of her crew were killed.

Knorr rescued forty-three survivors and treated them well, holding a funeral service for their dead shipmates and handing out cigarettes and cigars. Later in the day he sank a small Danish steamer carrying pit props, which were contraband. His luck, however, was about to run out. *Meteor* had been observed laying her mines and in London the Admiralty reacted quickly. Two light cruiser squadrons were ordered after her from Rosyth while a third, which had been carrying out a sweep off Norway, was ordered to cut off her escape. Luckily, at 08.30 on 9 August Knorr was warned by a vigilant Zeppelin airship that British cruisers were closing in on him. When the enemy's smoke appeared on the horizon he commandeered a Swedish fishing boat and scuttled the *Meteor*. He generously allowed his British prisoners to transfer to another neutral vessel from which they were rescued by the cruisers, and even gave their senior surviving officer seven pounds in British currency so that his men could replace any necessary items that had been lost aboard *The Ramsey*. After living on a diet of raw fish and potatoes he and his crew reached Germany safely.

The next raider to leave was the *Mowe* (Seagull), formerly a banana boat named *Pungo*. Twice the size of the *Meteor*, she was armed with four 5.9-inch guns, one 4.1-inch gun and four torpedo tubes, all cunningly concealed, and was also equipped to lay 500 mines. Under the command of Lieutenant Commander Count Nikolaus zu Dohna-Schlodien, formerly navigating officer aboard the battleship *Posen*, she left the Elbe on 29 December 1915 and, flying Swedish colours, headed north along the Norwegian coast, the traditional route taken by German ships seeking to avoid the British blockade. She passed through the British patrol line without incident and turned west to lay a minefield off the western entrance to the Pentland Firth. It was some time before Dohna was informed that his mines had claimed the pre-dreadnought battleship *King Edward VII*, on her way to Belfast for a refit, or that two merchant ships, the *Bayo* and the *Belgica*, had fallen victim to a second minefield he laid off La Rochelle.

During this, her first cruise, *Mowe* captured and sank another fifteen ships. Here it is only possible to relate the more remarkable of her adventures. Her first capture, on 11 January 1916, was the Ellerman liner *Farringford*, a remarkable coincidence as *Mowe* was herself disguised in the Ellerman colours. On the same day the collier *Corbridge* was taken and employed as a tender to replenish the raider's supply at pre-arranged rendezvous points. On 15 January it was the turn of the Elder Dempster liner *Appam*. She was carrying a cargo of rubber and copra, while among her passengers was the Governor of Sierra Cameroon. An unexpected surprise was a consignment of bullion with estimated contemporary value of £50,000. As *Mowe* was becoming over-crowded, Dohna decided to keep her with him for the moment and transfer his prisoners to her accommodation.

On 16 January, south of Madeira, the defensively armed merchant ship *Clan Mactavish* refused either to heave to or cease transmitting with her radio. Instead, her Scottish master decided to make a fight of it with his single 6-pounder gun. It was a very one-sided duel in which he only surrendered when nineteen of his crew had been killed and his engines were wrecked. Dohna shook the Scotsman's hand, criticised his reckless behaviour and told him that had their positions been reversed he would have done the same. But for a most unusual oversight, Dohna's own career might have ended shortly afterwards. The *Clan Mactavish's* raider signal had been picked up aboard the British cruiser *Essex* yet, incredibly, the signal was not passed to the decoding officer. Thus, as there were several British cruisers in the area, a golden opportunity to destroy a very dangerous raider was missed. Shortly after this the *Appam* was despatched to the United States with the crews of the captured merchantmen aboard, under the guard of a German prize crew. Seven more ships were captured after the *Clan Mactavish,* one of them, the *Westburn*, being despatched to Santa Cruz in the Canary Islands with the remainder of the raider's civilian captives aboard. Her presence was detected by the British armed merchant cruiser *Sutlej*, which pointedly remained outside the harbour. As there was no escape for *Westburn* she was scuttled and her prize crew were interned by the Spanish authorities.

The last capture of the cruise was the *Saxon Prince*, taken on 25 February 1916. *Mowe* then headed for home, bad weather and poor visibility enabling her to slip through the blockade and enter Wilhelmshaven on 5 March, triumphantly flying the house flags of her victims. Excluding the mine casualties, she had sunk fifteen ships with a total displacement exceeding 60,000 tons. She received a hero's welcome, including a parade by the entire ship's company past cheering crowds in the streets of Berlin. Dohna was rewarded by the Kaiser with the *Pour le Merite* while his officers and men received the Iron Cross Second Class.

In July, renamed *Vineta*, she undertook a brief cruise on the Baltic but only took one prize. After refitting and reverting to her original name she left for her second long range cruise on late November. This lasted until March 1917 and was equally successful, capturing twenty-five Allied or neutral ships of various nationalities carrying contraband. Of these twenty-three were sunk, the largest being the White Star liner *Georgic* of 10,077 tons. One of the cruellest aspects of the war at sea was the fate of horses in transit to the Allied armies. A large number had formed part of the *Georgic's* cargo and as there was no way of saving them they shared the fate of the ship. On 10 and 14 March 1917 two defensively armed merchantmen, respectively the *Otaki* and the *Governor*, fought back but were seriously out-gunned and sunk. Two more, the *Yarrowdale* and *Saint Theodore*, were considered suitable for conversion to raiders. The former's cargo consisted of 100 motor vehicles and several thousand tons of steel, too useful to be sent to the bottom, and she was sent off to Germany where she became the raider *Leopard*. The latter was subsequently armed at sea with two of the *Mowe's* guns and a radio, becoming the raider *Geier* (Vulture).

A captured Japanese freighter, the *Hudson Maru*, accompanied *Mowe* during the early days of 1917 as an accommodation ship and on 10 January was sent into Pernambuco with 250 prisoners aboard. A week later *Mowe* met the *Geier*, whose conversion had not been a success. Her only sinking was a 215-ton schooner and she was almost out of coal. A heavy sea was running, making it almost impossible to coal her from the *Mowe* and Dohna ordered her to be scuttled.

On 10 March there took place one of the most remarkable single ship duels of the entire war. The New Zealand Shipping Company's refrigerated meat ship *Otaki* was sailing in ballast from London to New York under the command of Captain Archibald Bisset Smith, a native of Aberdeen. Some 350 miles east of the Azores *Mowe* appeared over the horizon and for a while seemed content to keep *Otaki* under observation but at 14.30 signalled her to stop. Smith had no intention of doing anything of the kind and ordered his defensive armament, a single 4.7-inch gun, mounted on the stern, to open fire. It did so, hitting the raider, and kept hitting her hard. For once, Dohna and his crew had been caught on the hop. In spite of the serious damage being inflicted on their ship they quickly recovered and replied with the considerable armoury at their disposal – four 5.9-inch, one 4.1-inch and two 22-pounder guns. *Otaki* withstood this sort of punishment for two long hours at the end of which she was ablaze from stem to stern. Having lost six of his crew killed, Captain Smith ordered the boats to be lowered. Shortly after, the ship rolled over and sank rapidly by the stern, still flying her Merchant Marine red ensign. Captain Smith had refused to leave her.

The survivors were picked up from their boats by the raider, which had herself taken tremendous punishment as well as losing six men killed and ten wounded. The situation aboard her is described by her gunnery officer, Lieutenant Commander Jung.

Now the reports came chasing in from out battle stations. Water was pouring in forward, there was an extensive fire in the engine room bunker, and a revolt on the part of the prisoners – we had 338 white prisoners in the after hold that had been fitted out as prison quarters and 104 Indian lascars in the engine room bunkers – had already been suppressed during the engagement. But our position down by the head and our strong list were a source of anxiety, and thick smoke and glowing flames were bursting out from the engine room. After trying the collision mats – which were as good as useless – we managed to force heavy wedges of wood into the holes (in the hull) and stuff the gaps with sailcloth, so making her watertight in a rough and ready fashion. By flooding other compartments we corrected the list and brought her to an even keel. Midships the situation was even more serious. The burning coal bunkers could not extinguished. The bulkheads towards the bows was already heating and the planking began to smoulder. The midships section was sealed off and kept under live steam.

Ammunition, explosives and the warheads of torpedoes were manhandled onto the deck, ready to be heaved overboard if necessary. Throughout the night we remained stopped, waiting to see whether our smouldering volcano would erupt. The deck under my feet became hotter and hotter. By dawn the bulkheads were glowing and the paint began to peel off the hull. When flames appeared through melted caulking on the boat deck our situation had become desperate. Sea water was our only hope. Oxy-acetylene cutters bored holes in the hull at eleven suitable points. All available fire hydrants poured a flood of water into the mass of burning coal. Slowly, this became effective but because of the quantity of water we had poured into the ship she had settled even deeper. On top of everything, the pump valves became clogged with floating coal dust so that we wallowed helplessly in heavy seas. This dreadful state of affairs continued for two days until we got the better of the fire and flooding. Then, once again fit for action and in good heart, we turned north to face the risks of running the blockade on our passage to Germany.

On 13 March *Mowe* captured and sank the *Demeterton* and the following day ran down the *Governor* which, while approximately half the size of the *Otaki*, would not give in without a fight. Perhaps luckily for the seriously damaged raider this did not last long before her victim was also sent to the bottom. A week later *Mowe* reached Kiel, having safely passed through the blockade and turned south along the Norwegian coast. During her career as a raider she had captured, sunk or mined forty-four Allied ships, a total of 205,296 tons. Count Donha-Schlodien was honoured by being appointed Naval Aide to the Kaiser. Patched up, *Mowe* ended the war as a minelayer in the Baltic.

When details of the engagement between the *Mowe* and the *Otaki* became known in the United Kingdom there was a widespread demand that Captain Smith should be awarded the Victoria Cross, the country's highest award for bravery. The problem was that he was a civilian and members of the Mercantile Marine did not become eligible for the award until the rules of eligibility were changed by the

Royal Warrant of 22 May 1920. To circumvent the difficulty Smith was granted a backdated commission as a Lieutenant in the Royal Navy Reserve.

Something of a mystery surrounds the brief career of the Imperial Navy's third raider, the *Greif* (Griffin). Originally built with two funnels, she was disguised by removing one of them, painting Norwegian flags on her hull as well as the name *NORGE* (Norway) in large white letters. When she put to sea in February 1916 British naval intelligence was aware of the fact, possibly alerted by a visit paid to the ship before she set off by Prince Heinrich von Preussen, an unlikely honour to be conferred on an apparently nondescript tramp by a member of the Imperial Family. Three different groups were therefore despatched to hunt her down. On 29 February she was spotted steering north-east some 100 miles off the Norwegian coat by the armed merchant cruiser *Andes*. A second armed merchant cruiser, *Alcantara*, was ordered to investigate and instructed *Greif* to stop. As the raider complied her captain, a Commander Tietz, quietly ordered his gun crews to their action stations and continued to signal that he was a neutral heading for his home port. He was well aware that his four 150mm guns and one 105mm gun were no match for *Alcantara's* eight 6-inch and two 6-pounder guns and that with a maximum speed of 13 knots he could not hope to escape from the bigger ship. As *Alcantara* was hoisting out her boarding party's boat, Tietz gave the order to fire. His first salvo wrecked *Alcantara's* radio room and temporarily disabled her steering, but the armed merchant cruiser responded quickly and the two ships began hammering each other to destruction. In addition, *Greif* fired a torpedo from one of her submerged tubes and this inflicted fatal damage on her opponent, although she did not sink for some time. Meanwhile, *Andes* had joined the fray and the combined fire of both British ships turned *Greif* into a blazing wreck. Tietz ordered his men into their boats, after which *Andes* gave the raider her *coup de grâce*.

The fourth raider to be despatched was the *Wolf*, whose activities made her as famous as the *Mowe*. One of the remarkable things about her was her coal bunker capacity of 8,000 tons which, given an average speed of 8 knots, would give her a range of 32,000 miles. She also possessed the ability to change her appearance with a number of disguises. Her armament consisted of six 150mm guns, several smaller calibre guns and four submerged 500mm torpedo tubes. In addition, she carried 465 mines to be laid outside Allied harbours and a two-man Friedrichshafen FF.33 spotter plane named *Wolfchen* (Little Wolf) that gave her a much wider horizon.

After false starts caused by a bunker fire and fog, *Wolf* finally left Kiel on 30 November 1916 under Commander Karl Nerger. Her designated operation area was not the Atlantic but the Indian and Pacific Oceans. She evaded the blockade and passed through the Denmark Strait before turning south to pass down the middle of the Atlantic and round the Cape of Good Hope, where she laid some of her mines. Heading east then north, she laid more mines off Colombo and Bombay. Two British ships, *Worcestershire* and *Perseus*, fell victim to these with loss of life among the women and children aboard, provoking an angry response to the fact that no warning had been given of the presence of minefields.

Having left the area of Bombay, Nerger sailed south to a sort of maritime crossroads where the routes from South Africa to India crossed those from the East Indies to the Red Sea. On 27 February he made his first capture which, by a remarkable coincidence had, like *Wolf*, had once been owned by the Hansa Shipping Company. As *Gutenfels* she had been caught at Port Said on the outbreak of war and converted for British use as a tanker. Now she was called *Turritella* and sailed under the flag of the Anglo Saxon Petroleum Company Ltd. Nerger decided that she could be converted to the role of raider and armed her with a single 5.2mm gun and twenty-five mines. He changed her name again, this time to *Iltis* (Polecat) and now manned by a German crew, sent her to operate in the area around Aden. Her career as a raider lasted just a few days, for on 5 March, having disposed of her mines, she was intercepted by the British sloop *Odin*. As there could be no question of making a fight of it, her new commander scuttled her.

Meanwhile, on 1 March *Wolfchen* discovered the freighter *Jumna* and led *Wolf* to her. A shot across the bows brought her to a standstill but before the loaded port after gun could be traversed outboard there was a premature explosion in the breech. The result was that fourteen seamen on the raider's deck were either killed outright or sustained fatal wounds. *Wolfchen* was flying regularly about this time and on 11 March spotted another cargo vessel, the *Wordsworth*, east of the Seychelles and led *Wolf* to her. She was laden with rice and after *Wolf* had taken what she needed she was sunk with scuttling charges.

With the exception of a small barque sunk at the end of March, months were to pass before a worthwhile victim was to cross the raider's path. By then, *Wolf* had reached a point to the north-east of New Zealand. On 2 June *Wolfchen* spotted the New Zealand steamer *Wairuna* which was quickly intercepted. Her cargo included cheese, milk and meat among other items, which were welcomed by Nerger's crew. These items and 1,200 tons of coal were transferred to the *Wolf* and on 16 June her larder was further filled when *Wolfchen* brought in the schooner *Winslow*. Next day, having been thoroughly stripped, *Wairuna* was scuttled and *Winslow* was set adrift, a burning hulk.

Nerger now turned his attention to laying many of his mines along the coast of New Zealand, in the Cook Strait, separating the North and South Islands, and off the south-east coast of Australia, including a field off Gabo Island. These accounted for the 9,000-ton freighter *Cumberland* on 6 July.

In other respects, July was not productive. Two small vessels were captured and subsequently disposed of but by the end of the month *Wolf* was dangerously short of coal and provisions for her crew and the 200 prisoners she had aboard. Then, on 28 July Nerger's radio operators picked up a transmission in clear from the Burns Philp Company, which had extensive shipping interests throughout the Pacific and the Far East. The recipient remained unknown but was almost certainly in Rabaul on the island of New Britain. The message indicated that the Company's ship *Matanga* was on her way from Sydney and would arrive off Rabaul on 6 August with, among other things, 500 tons of good quality coal. *Wolfchen* was launched and spotted *Matanga* at 19.45 that evening, returning to the raider after signalling her position. At 07.00 next morning the seaplane was off again and, having located *Matanga*, ordered her to stop. As soon as *Wolf* caught up a boarding party was sent across, astonishing the freighter's captain with the request that he should confirm that he had 500 tons of coal aboard. Also aboard, and much appreciated by *Wolf's* officers, was the Rabaul business community's monthly order for hard liquor.

For the next week the two ships sailed in company to a sheltered harbour on Waigeo Island to the north of New Guinea and just south of the Equator. It was beautiful but unbearably hot, humid, airless and unhealthy, swarming with malaria-carrying mosquitoes after dark. For twelve days *Wolf's* crew worked on their ship, carrying out maintenance on the boilers and engines and scraping her bottom as well as transferring provisions and coal from the *Matanga*. At the end of this time both ships headed thankfully out into the clear air of the open sea, where *Matanga* was scuttled.

Wolf was now on her way home. Her route took her into the Coral Sea then, on the night of 2/3 September, through the Lombok Strait, where the last of her mines were laid, and on into the Indian Ocean. On 23 September *Wolfchen* took off on a scouting mission, returning within the hour to report a large merchant ship in the area of the Maldive Islands. Before long, the funnel smoke of the 7,000-ton Japanese cargo/passenger liner *Hitachi Maru* came into view. Closing the gap steadily, Nerger broke out his colours, signalled her to stop and then fired warning shots across her bows when she failed to respond. Simultaneously, he noted that men were working round a gun mounted on her stern. There was no response to his order and he opened fire before the Japanese could bring their own gun into action, slamming four salvos into the other ship, killing fourteen of her crew and wounding a further six. This brought the required response and a boarding party was sent across. It discovered a cargo that included silk, copper and brass, all commodities that were essential to the German war effort. The liner's passengers and crew were added to the already crowded conditions aboard the *Wolf*. Her commander, a Captain Tominaga, while not a member of either of Japan's armed services, nevertheless seemed to consider himself bound by the ethics of *bushido* in which the very concept of surrender was so alien that those who did were regarded as being beyond the limits of decent Japanese society. Deeply depressed by what had happened, he jumped overboard to his death shortly after.

For the moment both ships sailed together on a south-westerly course until 6 November when the *Hitachi Maru* was scuttled. For the moment *Wolfchen*, which had performed such valuable service throughout the voyage, was unable to fly because her wing fabric was worn out. Various materials were tried in its place, with generally unsatisfactory results, until a solution was found with Japanese silk coated with a mixture of deck paint and lacquer. On 10 November a Spanish freighter, the *Igoz Mendi*, was stopped. While technically neutral she was carrying 5,000 tons of coal destined for the Royal Navy, which was, of course, contraband. Nerger decided to keep her with him to replenish his own bunkers as required. Both ships were painted grey in preparation for the passage north up the Atlantic.

One three-masted barque, the *John H. Kirby*, was sunk as the raider rounded the Cape of Good Hope, and another, the *Marechal Davout*, in the South Atlantic. Steady northwards progress was made with two halts for coaling. For the last of these *Wolfchen* was flown ahead to ensure that the Islhas de Trinidade anchorage was clear of Allied warships. On 4 January 1918 the Norwegian barque *Storebror*, sailing in ballast from Beira in Portuguese East Africa to Montevideo, was intercepted and sunk, an act of dubious legality as, while she had recently called at the territory of a combatant, she was a neutral sailing empty with no contraband aboard.

By 21 February 1918 *Wolf* and *Igotz Mendi* had reached the Norwegian coast and were running south along it. Unfortunately, a dense fog descended the following day and *Igotz Mendi* ran hard aground on the Danish coast. Her crew and prisoners were taken off by a Danish gunboat, the former to be interned and the latter to have their freedom restored. *Wolf's* luck held and she entered Kiel to cheering crowds lining the quayside. Nerger, whose use of *Wolfchen* had opened a new chapter in naval warfare, received the *Pour le Merite*, promotion to Captain and an appointment as Officer Commanding Armed Trawlers North Sea Division, a job for which there was unlikely to be fierce competition. His crew received the Iron Cross Second Class and were dispersed to other duties after the ship's company had marched through Berlin.

On 21 December 1916 a very different sort of raider had slipped down the River Weser and out into open water. She was the fully rigged, three-masted barque *Seeadler* (Sea Eagle), originally the American-owned *Pass of Balmaha* which had been intercepted by a British cruiser off the Norwegian coast. The cruiser's captain had his suspicions about the ship and ordered her to head for Kirkwall in the Orkneys for a detailed search with an officer and six marines left aboard. Contrary to the wishes of the American skipper, the British officer insisted that she should fly the Union Flag. On the way she was captured by *U-36*. The marines were locked up and the American captain was told to take his ship into Cuxhaven. On arrival, the Americans were permitted to leave for a neutral country and the barque became the property of the Imperial Navy. The German Admiralty's thinking at this time was that as providing coal for raiders at sea was becoming increasingly difficult, the use of a sailing ship equipped with an auxiliary diesel engine would not only reduce the problem but also attract little attention as so much of the world's maritime traffic still employed vessels of this type. It was decided, therefore, that the *Pass of Balmaha* would assume the identity of a neutral Norwegian ship and a great deal of effort into ensuring that even the smallest details would seem accurate to a boarding party. For example, the ship's navigational instruments all bore the name of a well-known Norwegian maker and the captain's cabin contained portraits of the Norwegian King and Queen and King Edward VII of Great Britain. In addition she carried false papers made out in the name of *Hero* and her German crew were all fluent in Norwegian or Swedish. Initially, her disguise was supplemented by a deck cargo of Norwegian timber, apparently bound for Australia. Her armament consisted of two carefully concealed 105mm guns, plus machine guns and rifles.

The Imperial Navy contained very few officers with experience in sail, but *Seeadler* was commanded by one of the most remarkable officers in the service. Lieutenant Commander Count Felix von Luckner was born in 1881 and had run away to sea when he was twelve. Since then he had gained a wide experience in sail and obtained his Mate's ticket, changing to steam in 1908. He had obtained a reserve commission in the Imperial Navy and since being called up in 1914 he had seen active service at the Battles of Heligoland Bight and Jutland. Luckner's principal characteristics were an engaging personality that made him a favourite of the Kaiser's, and a fertile – some would say cunning – mind that would enable him to outwit his opponents time and again, resulting in his being nicknamed The Sea Devil.

Seeadler did not break through the British blockade. On Christmas Day 1916 she was stopped by the Armed Merchant Cruiser *Avenger*. The 'Norwegian' seamen were, of course, dressed in civilian seagoing rig and to add a touch of authenticity Luckner provided female attire and a blonde wig for a young sailor, who played the part of his wife. Satisfied, the two British officers in the boarding party returned to their own ship and *Seeadler* went on her way, ditching her timber deck cargo as soon as she was alone.

The raider's career took her from the Atlantic into the Pacific and lasted until 2 August 1917. She did not cause the Allies too much damage, capturing just sixteen ships with a total displacement of only 30,099 tons. Just three ships displaced over 3,000 tons and most of the remainder were sailing ships displacing between 364 and 2,199 tons, including three American schooners. This was not unduly impressive and its interest lies in the manner of their capture and Luckner's ability to avoid his pursuers, which latterly included the United States Navy. Sometimes, when approaching a steamer, he would request a time check as a navigational aid, a common enough request made by sailing ships. The steamer would slow down to oblige. Then *Seeadler* would send up the Imperial Navy's ensign, fire a shot across her victim's bows, and that would be that. On another occasion he impertinently took his capture into Rio de Janeiro himself and acquired supplies on her owner's account. Sometimes flotsam bearing *Seeadler's* name would be thrown overboard to give the impression that she had sunk.

A further ruse was to set off a smoke discharger on his deck and request assistance in extinguishing the 'fire' from his potential victim, which was then snapped up. By March 1917 he had over 200 prisoners aboard and they were eating their way through the ship's food supplies at an unacceptable rate. On 21 March he took the large French barque *Cambronne* and decided to send them off in her. She would be manned by her own crew, which he knew would immediately disclose his presence as soon as they reached port, so he removed her topgallant masts and destroyed spars and sails that could be employed as a replacements. This meant that the *Cambronne* could only sail slowly and that by the time she reached port *Seeadler* would be far away. His method of stopping sailing ships that were faster than his own was simple. His machine guns would fire continuously into her sails until they were full of holes and no longer able to hold the wind. Then, inevitably, she would slow down and be overhauled and threatened with heavier weapons unless she surrendered. There seemed to be no end to Luckner's ingenuity yet, throughout *Seeadler's* career, only one life was lost, and that because of an accident.

By summer it was becoming clear that *Seeadler* was in dire need of careening so Luckner took her to Mopelia Island, some 280 miles from Tahiti, hoping that she could be heeled over and scraped in the shelter of its large lagoon. Unfortunately, the entrance to the lagoon was too shallow and *Seeadler* was forced to anchor outside the coral reef. According to Luckner, on 2 August she was driven onto the reef, wrecked and dismasted by what today we would call a tsunami. There is no official record of this kind of activity in the region in August 1917, and some American prisoners later stated that most of the crew were ashore enjoying themselves and that the ship had simply run herself aground, possibly as a result of dragging her anchor. Quite possibly Luckner, a notable teller of tall tales, was doing his best to save face. The subsequent story of his own and his crew's adventures was one of escapes and recaptures that would do justice to any Hollywood script but one which shortage of space prevents the telling here.

It will be recalled that when the British freighter *Yarrowdale* was captured by the *Mowe* she was sent to Germany for conversion to the role of commerce raider and renamed *Leopard*. The work was carried out at the Kaiserliche Werft yard in Kiel, from which she emerged with the comparatively heavy armament of five 150mm and four 88mm guns and two torpedo tubes. At the beginning of March 1917 she sailed on her first and only mission under the command of Lieutenant Commander Hans von Laffert, disguised as the Norwegian freighter *Rena*, the words *RENA* and *NORGE* being painted on either side of her hull, together with the Norwegian flag. She did not get very far and on 16 March ran into the armoured cruiser *Achilles* and the armed boarding vessel *Dundee* under the command, respectively, of Captain F.M. Leake and Commander Selwyn M. Day, in the area of the Faroe Islands.

Leake ordered her to proceed west by south for a detailed examination by *Dundee*. At 14.40, as the raider was closing in on *Dundee*, Day signalled WHAT SHIP IS THAT? There was no reply and five minutes later he flashed a second signal: STOP INSTANTLY. This drew the response AP, which was simply gibberish. PAY ATTENTION TO MY SIGNALS ordered Day. Again, there was no reply and at 14.50 he ordered a blank round to be fired. Nine minutes later he asked WHAT IS YOUR CARGO? and received the reply GENERAL.

A boat containing a boarding party consisting of one officer and five ratings had been despatched at 14.42 but was no longer visible, being in the lee of the stranger. The easygoing attitudes that had resulted in the loss of *The Ramsey* and the *Alcantara* had long gone. Day's crew were at action stations and he had positioned *Dundee* so that her broadside was across the raider's stern. Laffert was perfectly aware that his ship could be raked, with terrible consequences, and that he could make little or no reply with his own guns. By using his port or starboard screws he tried to improve his position but Day correctly interpreted the water disturbance created by the propellers and adjusted his own position accordingly. *Leopard's* behaviour, her appearance, the information contained in his confidential books and the lack of communication from his boarding party all reinforced Day's suspicion that she was a raider. At 15.10 he signalled WHERE

ARE YOU FROM? The answer MOBILE came back. That seemed improbable but he decided to wait a little longer. At 15.30, still not having heard from the boarding party, he decided to test the other's veracity, signalling WHEN DID YOU LEAVE? There was no reply.

Laffert, unable to calculate the time required for the voyage, knew that he had been found out and decided to make the best of it. Ten minutes later Day was alerted by an unusual noise. One of the raider's Norwegian flags, painted on large boards hinged at the bottom, had fallen outboard. The aperture within could only contain guns and he immediately gave the order to fire. *Leopard* was now turning slowly to port to bring her own broadside to bear but Day responding by ordering half-ahead to deny any such advantage. Hardly had *Dundee* began to gather way than two torpedoes sped 20 to 50 feet past her stern.

Dundee's guns were now hammering away at 1,000 yards range. Forty-four 4-inch and twenty-five 3-pounder rounds had been fired before *Leopard* got off her first shot. 'Every shot was a hit,' wrote Day in his report.

> The first (from our aft 4-inch) raked her port battery deck, causing an explosion and volumes of smoke. The fore gun fired through the deck into her engine room and volumes of steam spread with intense smoke and flames caused by further hits, so as to completely the ship from us from bridge to stern. The 3-pounder gun fired at her bridge. *Dundee* was then in the smoke to leeward and both ships were practically obscured from each other in consequence. Observing *Achilles* on an almost opposite bearing, I turned and went to full speed and down the lane of smoke so as to clear the range for the cruiser. On turning, one torpedo was fired at us, and also three salvoes, two short and one over, of three or four guns by her port broadside. There followed some very wild single shots, including shrapnel, fragments of the latter only hitting the ship. The aft gun was bearing and made consistently excellent on any visible part of the enemy. Ignited oil was observed streaming from her port beam.

Meanwhile, *Achilles* had joined in the fray at 5,300 yards as soon as it had started. 'The raider was firing at her,' recorded Captain Leake, 'but with more intensity at *Dundee,* whose safety was due to the prompt manner in which Commander Day answered the raider's first hostile act, and the initial success she gained in getting raking hits; hers was a most dangerous position and she extracted herself with the utmost credit.

'On opening fire the raider at once enveloped herself in smoke of a light colour. At 15.55 she fired a torpedo at *Achilles,* which broke surface off the port quarter. Hits were now being obtained and the raider was on fire forward. About this time she was hit in the bow (on the gripe) by a torpedo from *Achilles.*'

By 16.10 *Dundee* had expended all her ammunition. *Leopard* had become a floating inferno but continued to fight with one gun. Finally, at 16.33, the raider finally succumbed to *Achilles'* fire, listed slightly to port and sank horizontally. There were no survivors and the fate of *Dundee's* boarding party remains unknown; presumably, once aboard the raider they were overpowered and then confined during the action. In other respects, there were no British casualties.

Leopard was the last commerce raider to be sent out by the Imperial Navy. A small number of raiders had achieved spectacular success, others had produced modest results, and some had barely justified their conversion costs. The fact was that they were too few in number and the world's oceans too vast for them to make any difference. While, with the exception of some peripheral activity in the Baltic and at the northern and southern extremities of the North Sea, the High Seas Fleet had rotted at its mooring since Jutland, the U-boat arm had brought the United Kingdom to the verge of starvation until the tide was turned by the introduction of escorted ocean convoys in May 1917.

Index